Table of Contents

MY FREE GIFT TO YOU! 6

>> GET THE FULL ITALIAN ONLINE COURSE WITH AUDIO LESSONS << 7

INTRODUCTION: ARE YOU READY FOR AN AMAZING JOURNEY? 8

PART 1: LET'S GET STARTED 12
CHAPTER 1: LETTERS & FONETIC 13
CHAPTER 2: NUMBERS 15

PART 2: GETTING DOWN TO BUSINESS 18
CHAPTER 3: PERSONAL PRONOUNS 19
CHAPTER 4: VERBS (-ARE, -ERE, -IRE) 20
CHAPTER 5: GREETINGS AND INTRODUCTIONS 26
CHAPTER 6: ARTICLES 30
CHAPTER 7: COLOURS 33
CHAPTER 8: ADJECTIVES 36
CHAPTER 9: THE VERB "TO HAVE" TO TELL YOUR AGE 47
CHAPTER 10: THE WEATHER, THE MONTHS, AND THE DAYS OF THE WEEK 52
CHAPTER 11: THE CLOCK (L'OROLOGIO) 58
CHAPTER 12: ASKING QUESTIONS: WHO, WHAT, WHEN, WHERE... 66
CHAPTER 13: MODAL VERBS (VERBI MODALI) 68
CHAPTER 14: REFLEXIVE VERBS (VERBI RIFLESSIVI) 71
CHAPTER 15: WHERE IS IT? (DOV'È?) 74
CHAPTER 16: POSSESSIVE ADJECTIVES 79
CHAPTER 17: DEMONSTRATIVE ADJECTIVES 82
CHAPTER 18: I LIKE IT! (MI PIACE) 84
CHAPTER 19: PAST TENSE: PASSATO PROSSIMO & PASSATO REMOTO 86
CHAPTER 20: FUTURE TENSE (FUTURO SEMPLICE) 95

PART 3: USEFUL VOCABULARY 98
CHAPTER 21: HEALTH AND THE BODY 99
CHAPTER 22: MY CLOTHES 104
CHAPTER 23: MY HOUSE 109
CHAPTER 24: AT THE RESTAURANT 111

CHAPTER 25: TRAVEL AND HOLIDAYS..118

CONCLUSION: NOW, EMBARK ON YOUR OWN ADVENTURE!..................123

>> GET THE FULL ITALIAN ONLINE COURSE WITH AUDIO LESSONS << 124

PS: CAN I ASK YOU A QUICK FAVOR?..125

PREVIEW OF "ITALIAN FOR TOURISTS - THE MOST ESSENTIAL ITALIAN
GUIDE TO TRAVEL ABROAD, MEET PEOPLE & FIND YOUR WAY AROUND -
ALL WHILE SPEAKING PERFECT ITALIAN!" 126

CHECK OUT MY OTHER BOOKS 146

ABOUT THE AUTHOR 147

LEARN ITALIAN IN 7 DAYS!

The Ultimate Crash Course to Learning the Basics of the Italian Language in No Time

By Dagny Taggart

Disclaimer

The information provided in this book is designed to provide helpful information on the subjects discussed. The author's books are only meant to provide the reader with the basics knowledge of a certain language, without any warranties regarding whether the student will, or will not, be able to incorporate and apply all the information provided. Although the writer will make her best effort share her insights, language learning is a difficult task, and each person needs a different timeframe to fully incorporate a new language. This book, nor any of the author's books constitute a promise that the reader will learn a certain language within a certain timeframe.

Dedicated to those who love going beyond their own frontiers.

Keep on traveling,

Dagny Taggart

My FREE Gift to You!

As a way of saying thank you for downloading my book, I'd like to send you an exclusive gift that will revolutionize the way you learn new languages. It's an extremely comprehensive PDF with 15 language hacking rules that **will help you learn 300% <u>faster</u>, with <u>less effort</u>, and with <u>higher than ever retention rates</u>**.

This guide is an amazing complement to the book you just got, and could easily be a stand-alone product, but for now I've decided to give it away for free, to thank you for being such an awesome reader, and to make sure I give you all the value that I can to help you succeed faster on your language learning journey.

To get your FREE gift, go to the link below, write down your email address and I'll send it right away!

>> <u>http://bit.ly/ItalianGift</u><<

GET **INSTANT** ACCESS

>> Get The Full Italian Online Course With Audio Lessons <<

If you truly want to learn Italian 300% FASTER, then hear this out.

I've partnered with the most revolutionary language teachers to bring you the very best Italian online course I've ever seen. It's a mind-blowing program specifically created for language hackers such as ourselves. It will allow you learn Italian 3x faster, straight from the comfort of your own home, office, or wherever you may be. It's like having an unfair advantage!

The Online Course consists of:

+ 183 Built-In Lessons
+ 95 Interactive Audio Lessons
+ 24/7 Support to Keep You Going

The program is extremely engaging, fun, and easy-going. You won't even notice you are learning a complex foreign language from scratch. And before you realize it, by the time you go through all the lessons you will officially become a truly solid Italian speaker.

Old classrooms are a thing of the past. It's time for a language revolution.

If you'd like to go the extra mile, follow the link below and let the revolution begin!

>> http://www.bitly.com/Italian-Course <<

CHECK OUT THE COURSE »

I

Introduction
Are You Ready for an Amazing Journey?

Most people are daunted by the idea of learning a language. They think it's impossible, even unfathomable. I remember as a junior in high school, watching footage of Jackie O giving a speech in French. I was so impressed and inspired by the ease at which she spoke this other language of which I could not understand one single word.

At that moment, I knew I had to learn at least one foreign language. I started with Italian, later took on Mandarin, and most recently have started learning Portuguese. No matter how challenging and unattainable it may seem, millions of people have done it. You do NOT have to be a genius to learn another language. You DO have to be willing to take risks and make mistakes, sometimes even make a fool of yourself, be dedicated, and of course, practice, practice, practice!

This book will only provide you with the basics in order to get started learning the Italian language. It is geared towards those who are planning to travel to a Italian-speaking country and covers many common scenarios you may find yourself in so feel free to skip around to the topic that is most prudent to you at the moment.

I will now list some tips that I have found useful and should be very helpful to you in your journey of learning Italian. I don't wish you luck because that will not get you anywhere- reading this book, dedicating yourself, and taking some risks will!

Important note

Due to the nature of this book (it contains charts, graphs, and so on), you will better your reading experience by setting your device on *LANDSCAPE* mode!

Language Tips

Tip #1 - Keep an Open Mind

It may seem obvious but you must understand that languages are very different from each other. You cannot expect them to translate word for word. *'There is a black dog'* will not translate word for word with the same word order in Italian. You have to get used to the idea of translating WHOLE ideas. So don't find yourself saying, *"Why is everything backwards in Italian?"* because it may seem that way many times.   Keep your mind open to the many differences that you will find in the language that go far beyond just the words.

Tip #2 - Take Risks

Be fearless. Talk to as many people as you can. The more practice you get the better and don't worry about looking like a fool when you say, *"I am pregnant"* rather than *"I am embarrassed,"* which as you will find out can be a common mistake. If anyone is laughing remember they are not laughing at you. Just laugh with them, move on, and LEARN from it, which brings us to our next tip.

Tip #3 - Learn from your Mistakes

It doesn't help to get down because you made one more mistake when trying to order at a restaurant, take a taxi, or just in a friendly conversation. Making mistakes is a HUGE part of learning a language. You have to put yourself out there as we said and be willing to make tons of mistakes! Why? Because what can you do with mistakes. You can LEARN from them. If you never make a mistake, you probably are not learning as much as you could. So every time you mess up when trying to communicate, learn from it, move on, and keep your head up!

Tip #4 - Immerse yourself in the language

If you're not yet able to go to a Italian-speaking country, try to pretend that you are. Surround yourself with Italian. Listen to music in Italian, watch movies, TV shows, in Italian. Play games on your phone, computer, etc. in Italian. Another great idea is to actually put your phone, computer, tablet and/or other electronic devices in Italian. It can be frustrating at first but in the end this exposure will definitely pay off.

Tip #5 - Start Thinking in Italian

I remember being a senior in high school and working as a lifeguard at a fairly deserted pool. While I was sitting and staring at the empty waters, I would speak to myself or think to myself (to not seem so crazy) in Italian. I would describe my surroundings, talk about what I had done and what I was going to do, etc. While I was riding my bike, I would do the same thing. During any activity when you don't need to talk or think about anything else, keep your brain constantly going in Italian to get even more practice in the language. So get ready to turn off the English and jumpstart your Italian brain!

Tip #6 - Label your Surroundings/Use Flashcards

When I started to learn Portuguese, I bought an excellent book that included stickers so that you could label your surroundings. So I had stickers all over my parents' house from the kitchen to the bathroom that labeled the door, the dishes, furniture, parts of the house, etc. It was a great, constant reminder of how to say these objects in another language. You can just make your own labels and stick them all over the house and hope it doesn't bother your family or housemates too much!

Tip #7 - Use Context clues, visuals, gestures, expressions, etc.

If you don't understand a word that you have heard or read, look or listen to the surrounding words and the situation to help you. If you are in a restaurant and your friend says, "I am going to ??? a sandwich." You can take a guess that she said *order* or *eat* but you don't have to understand every word in order to understand the general meaning. When you are in a conversation use gestures, expressions, and things around you to help communicate your meaning. Teaching English as a second language to young learners taught me this. If you act everything out, you are more likely to get your point across. If you need to say the word *bird* and you don't know how you can start flapping your arms and chirping and then you will get your point across and possibly learn how to say *bird*. It may seem ridiculous but as I said, you have to be willing to look silly to learn another language and this greatly helps your language communication and learning.

Tip #8 - Circumlocution

Circumlo... what? This is just a fancy word for describing something when you don't know how to say it. If you are looking to buy an umbrella and don't know how to say it, what can you do? You can describe it using words you know. You can say, it is something used for the rain that opens and closes and then hopefully someone will understand you, help you, and maybe teach you how to say this word. Using circumlocution is excellent language practice and is much better than just giving up when you don't know how to say a word. So keep talking even if you have a limited vocabulary. Say what you can and describe or act out what you can't!

PART 1

LET'S GET STARTED

Chapter 1
Letters & Fonetic

The Italian alphabet consists of 21 letters plus 5 foreign letters: J (i lunga) K (cappa) W (doppia vu / vu doppia) X (ics) Y (ipsilon).

ALFABETO - alphabet

A - a	H - acca	O – o	U - u
B - bi	I – i	P - pi	V - vu
C - ci	J - i lunga	Q - qu	W - vu doppia
D - di	k - cappa	R - erre	X - ics
E - e	L - elle	S - esse	Y - ipsilon
F - effe	M - emme	T - ti	Z- zeta
G – gi	N - enne		

Here you can see the pronunciation of the Italian vowels:

VOCALI – vowels	PRONUNCIA - PRONUNCIATION	ESEMPI INGLESI – english examples
a	[a]	cat
e	[e] [ɛ]	ready bed
i	[i]	thing
o	[o] [ɔ]	call lot
u	[u]	food

Some of the consonants have different sounds depending on the preceding or following letters:

CONSONANT – consonants	PRONUNCIA - pronunciation	ESEMPI INGLESI – english examples

C		
C + a / o / u; ch + e; ch + i	[ka / ko / ku]; [ke / kɛ]; [ki]	Car; Chemistry; kick
C + e; c + i	[tʃe]; [tʃi]	Cherry; chip
Ci + a; Ci + o; Ci + u	[tʃa]; [tʃo]; [tʃu]	Chance; choice; chew
CONSONANT – consonants	PRONUNCIA - PRONUNCIATION	ESEMPI INGLESI – english examples
G		
g + a / o / u; gh + e; gh + i	[ga / go / gu]; [ge / gɛ]; [gi]	Gun; Game; give
g + e; g + i	[dʒe]; [dʒi]	Gentle; ginger
gi + a; gi + o; gi + u	[dʒa]; [dʒo]; [dʒu]	Jar; Job; july
g + li	ʎ	(a bit like "billion", or the Spanish "ll")
gli	[gli]	glimmer
gn	[ɲ]	(a bit like "menu", but stronger)

S		
sc + e; sc + i	[ʃe]; [ʃi]	share; shift
sci + a / o / u	[ʃa / o / u]	Shut; show; shoot
sc + consonant	[sk]	school

Chapter 2
Numbers

Cardinal numbers

0	Zero	21	Ventuno
1	Uno	22	Ventidue
2	Due	23	Ventitré
3	Tre	24	Ventiquattro
4	Quattro	25	Venticinque
5	Cinque	26	Ventisei
6	Sei	27	Ventisette
7	Sette	28	Ventotto
8	Otto	29	Ventinove
9	Nove	30	Trenta
10	Dieci	40	Quaranta
11	Undici	50	Cinquanta
12	Dodici	60	Sessanta
13	Tredici	70	Settanta
14	Quattordici	80	Ottanta
15	Quindici	90	Novanta
16	Sedici	100	Cento
17	Diciassette	1000	Mille
18	Diciotto	10000	Diecimila
19	Diciannove	100000	Centomila
20	Venti	1000000	Un milione
		1000000000	Un miliardo

Ordinal numbers

1°	primo
2°	secondo
3°	terzo
4°	quarto
5°	quinto
6°	sesto
7°	settimo
8°	ottavo
9°	nono
10°	decimo
11°	undicesimo
12°	dodicesimo
13°	tredicesimo
14°	quattordicesimo
15°	quindicesimo
16°	sedicesimo
17°	diciassettesimo
18°	diciottesimo
19°	diciannovesimo
20°	ventesimo
100°	centesimo

Test Your Italian!

1) Write the correct numbers in letters

1. The man who win a competition in the 1° = ...
2. The last one out of 50 people is the 50° = ...

3. 4-1 = ……………….
4. 110- 87 = ……………….
5. The last number formed by two numbers is ……………….

Answers

1. PRIMO
2. CINQUANTESIMO
3. TRE
4. VENTITRE
5. *NOVANTANOVE*

PART 2

GETTING DOWN TO BUSINESS

Chapter 3
Personal pronouns

In Italian there are 6 forms to address a person in an informal situation, plus 1 to adress in formal situations:

I → IO
You → TU
He → EGLI* / LUI
She → ELLA* / LEI
We → NOI
You → VOI
They → ESSI* (masculine) / ESSE* (feminine)

*Children at school study the forms "egli / ella - essi / esse", but generally speaking nobody uses them, preferring the other forms "LUI = he"; "LEI = she" and "LORO = they".

The formal pronoun is LEI and it can be used both to talk about a woman who is not here (she), and to a present person (both a man and a woman) in a formal situation (you); in both cases the verb is in the same form, e.g.:

1) If you are talking to your friend about a man that is going to sit down on a chair, you will say:

IL SIGNORE (LUI) È STANCO   The gentleman (he) is tired
LA SIGNORA (LEI) È STANCA   The lady (she) is tired

2) If you want to make sure that they are tired, you can ask them:

SIGNORE, LEI È STANCO?   Are you tired, sir?
SIGNORA, LEI È STANCA?   Are you tired, madam?

Chapter 4
Verbs (-are, -ere, -ire)

Regular verbs (I VERBI REGOLARI)

Italian has three conjugations: verbs may end in -ARE, -ERE, and -IRE. Most of them belong to the firts conjugation (-ARE).

First conjugation (PARLARE – to speak)

IO	PARL-	O
TU	PARL-	I
LUI / LEI	PARL-	A
NOI	PARL-	IAMO
VOI	PARL-	ATE
LORO	PARL-	ANO

Second conjugation (VIVERE - to live)

IO	VIV-	O
TU	VIV-	I
LUI / LEI	VIV-	E
NOI	VIV-	IAMO
VOI	VIV-	ETE
LORO	VIV-	ONO

Third conjugation (DORMIRE - to sleep)

IO	DORM-	O
TU	DORM-	I
LUI / LEI	DORM-	E
NOI	DORM-	IAMO
VOI	DORM-	ITE
LORO	DORM-	ONO

Irregular Verbs (I VERBI IRREGOLARI)

There are some important irregular verbs, like to go (ANDARE), to do (FARE), to know (SAPERE), to go out (USCIRE), to understand (CAPIRE), that is necessary to learn:

	ANDARE	FARE	SAPERE	USCIRE	CAPIRE
IO	VADO	FACCIO	SO	ESCO	CAPISCO
TU	VAI	FAI	SAI	ESCI	CAPISCI
LUI / LEI	VA	FA	SA	ESCE	CAPISCE
NOI	ANDIAMO	FACCIAMO	SAPPIAMO	USCIAMO	CAPIAMO
VOI	ANDATE	FATE	SAPETE	USCITE	CAPITE
LORO	VANNO	FANNO	SANNO	ESCONO	CAPISCONO

Other verbs, like to prefer (PREFERIRE) and to finish (FINIRE) behave like the verb "CAPIRE", so you just need to say "PREFER-" or "FIN-", instead of "CAP-", and to add the same suffixes of the verb "CAPIRE".

Test Your Italian!

1) Conjugate the verbs.

1° conjugation	ABITARE	CAMMINARE	DOMANDARE	LAVORARE	ASCOLTARE
IO					
TU					
LUI / LEI					
NOI					
VOI					
LORO					

2° conjugation	PRENDERE	METTERE	RAGGIUNGERE	CHIEDERE	VEDERE
IO					

TU					
LUI / LEI					
NOI					
VOI					
LORO					

3° conjugation	APRIRE	SENTIRE	FINIRE	PREFERIRE	VESTIRE
IO					
TU					
LUI / LEI					
NOI					
VOI					
LORO					

2) Complete the sentences with the correct form of the verb.

1. Noi (aspettare) ………………………… l'autobus
2. Tu (aprire) ………………………… la porta
3. Lui (camminare) …………………………molto
4. Loro (ascoltare) ………………………… la radio
5. Io (abitare) ………………………… in Italia.
6. Lei (dormire) ………………………… fino a tardi
7. Voi (domandare) ………………………… quando non (capire) …………………………
8. Quando (tu)* (raggiungere) ………………………… la stazione, (chiedere) ………………………… quando (passare) ………………………… il treno
9. Noi (guardare) ………………………… la televisione tutte le sere.
10. A giugno (finire) ………………………… la scuola.

*The Italian language is a "null-subject language": it means that its grammar permits an independent clause to lack an explicit subject. Null-subject languages express person, number, and/or gender   agreement with the referent on the verb, rendering a subject noun phrase redundant. Thus in this sentence, you would not use the subject. You may say it if you want to emphasize the subject, e.g.: IO VADO A LETTO, (I go to bed) stresses the fact that it is me who goes to bed, I don't know what you want to do, but I go to bed.

3) Correct the mistakes when you find them.

1. Io ando al mare
2. Voi beviamo il caffè
3. Loro mangiate la torta al cioccolato
4. Lei parla molto bene italiano
5. Tu abita in America
6. Lui sai tre lingue
7. Noi ascoltano il telegiornale
8. Io non capire bene la matematica
9. Voi preferite il vino alla birra
10. Signor Rossi, sente quello che le dico?

4.3 The negative form NON

To negate a sentence, you have to write NON before the verb:

IO VADO AL CINEMA → IO **NON** VADO AL CINEMA

4) Change the following affirmative sentences into negative.

1. IO SO PARLARE ITALIANO →
2. A ME PIACE IL MARE →
3. IO HO UN FRATELLO →
4. LEI GUARDA UN FILM →
5. LORO GIOCANO A CALCIO →

Answers

Exercise 1

1° conj.	ABITARE	CAMMINARE	DOMANDARE	LAVORARE	ASCOLTARE
IO	ABITO	CAMMINO	DOMANDO	LAVORO	ASCOLTO
TU	ABITI	CAMMINI	DOMANDI	LAVORI	ASCOLTI
LUI / LEI	ABITA	CAMMINA	DOMANDA	LAVORA	ASCOLTA
NOI	ABITIAMO	CAMMINIAMO	DOMANDIAMO	LAVORIAMO	ASCOLTIAMO
VOI	ABITATE	CAMMINATE	DOMANDATE	LAVORATE	ASCOLTATE
LORO	ABITANO	CAMMINANO	DOMANDANO	LAVORANO	ASCOLTANO

2° conj.	PRENDERE	METTERE	RAGGIUNGERE	CHIEDERE	VEDERE
IO	PRENDO	METTO	RAGGIUNGO	CHIEDO	VEDO
TU	PRENDI	METTI	RAGGIUNGI	CHIEDI	VEDI
LUI / LEI	PRENDE	METTE	RAGGIUNGE	CHIEDE	VEDE
NOI	PRENDIAMO	METTIAMO	RAGGIUNGIAMO	CHIEDIAMO	VEDIAMO
VOI	PRENDETE	METTETE	RAGGIUNGETE	CHIEDETE	VEDETE
LORO	PRENDONO	METTONO	RAGGIUNGONO	CHIEDONO	VEDONO

3° conj.	APRIRE	SENTIRE	FINIRE	PREFERIRE	VESTIRE
IO	APRO	SENTO	FINISCO	PREFERISCO	VESTO
TU	APRI	SENTI	FINISCI	PREFERISCI	VESTI
LUI / LEI	APRE	SENTE	FINISCE	PREFERISCE	VESTE
NOI	APRIAMO	SENTIAMO	FINIAMO	PREFERIAMO	VESTIAMO
VOI	APRITE	SENTITE	FINITE	PREFERITE	VESTITE
LORO	APRONO	SENTONO	FINISCONO	PREFERISCONO	VESTONO

Exercise 2

1. Noi aspettiamo l'autobus
2. Tu apri   la porta
3. Lui cammina molto
4. Loro ascoltano la radio
5. Io abito in Italia.
6. Lei dorme fino a tardi
7. Voi domandate quando non capite
8. Quando raggiungi la stazione, chiedi quando passa il treno
11. Noi guardiamo la televisione tutte le sere.
12. A giugno finisce la scuola.

Exercise 3

1. Io vado al mare
2. Voi bevete il caffè
3. Loro mangiano la torta al cioccolato
4. Lei parla molto bene italiano
5. Tu abiti in America
6. Lui sa tre lingue
7. Noi ascoltiamo il telegiornale
8. Io non capisco bene la matematica
9. Voi preferite il vino alla birra
10. Signor Rossi, sente quello che le dico?

Exercise 4

1) IO NON SO PARLARE ITALIANO
2) A ME NON PIACE IL MARE
3) IO NON HO UN FRATELLO
4) LEI NON GUARDA UN FILM
5) LORO NON GIOCANO A CALCIO

Chapter 5
Greetings and Introductions

In the Italian language there are two ways to refer to a person you are talking to: TU, the informal way and LEI, the formal way (not to be confused with LEI, meaning "she"). If you are talking to family members, children, and close friends you can use the familiar forms, otherwise you will refer to your interlocutor with LEI, and also the verb needs to be conjugated according to the third singular person.

Formal meeting:

BUONGIORNO, COME STA? SALVE BUONA SERA	Good morning, how are you? Hello Good evening
BENE, GRAZIE, E LEI?	Fine, thanks. And what about you?
BENISSIMO, GRAZIE.	Very well, thank you.

Informal meeting:

CIAO! COME STAI? COME VA? COME TI SENTI?	Hi! How are you? How is it going? How do you feel?
BENE MALE NON MOLTO BENE / COSÌ COSÌ BENISSIMO	Fine / well Bad Not so well Very well
IO MI CHIAMO …. . E TU?	My name is … . What's your name?
IO SONO … . PIACERE	I am … . Nice to meet you.
PIACERE MIO	My pleasure
CIAO!	Bye!

5.1 IL VERBO STARE
IO   STO

TU	STAI
LUI / LEI	STA
NOI	STIAMO
VOI	STATE
LORO	STANNO

1) Complete the sentences:
A) .... Signor Rossi, come ....?
B)   :-) ...., grazie. E lei?
A) :-(......................., sono un po' stanco.

5.2 The verb "to be" _ IL VERBO ESSERE

IO	SONO
TU	SEI
(EGLI / ELLA) LUI / LEI	È
NOI	SIAMO
VOI	SIETE
(ESSI / ESSE) LORO	SONO

5.3 How are feeling?   _ COME TI SENTI?

Felice, Contento, Bene, Emozionato, In Gran Forma

Triste, Male

Malato/a, Sofferente

Arrabiato/a, Dispiaciuto/a

28

COSÌ COSÌ

Stanco/a

2) Complete the dialog with the right adjective:

A) CIAO LUCA, COME TI SENTI?
B)   MI SENTO F............., STO M............. B.............

A) BUONA SERA SIGNORA MARIA, COME STA?
B) BUONA SERA, IERI ERO UN PO' ....
MA OGGI SONO ....

A) SALVE ALESSANDRO, COME VA?
B) TUTTO ...., GRAZIE, E TE?
A) C....... C........ :   IERI ERO ...., MA ORA STO
MEGLIO.

3) Invent a dialog:
A)
B)
A)

Answers

Exercise 1

A) BUONGIORNO Signor Rossi, come STA?
B)   :-) BENE, grazie. E lei?
A) :-(MALE, sono un po' stanco.

A) CIAO LUCA, COME TI SENTI?

B)   MI SENTO FELICE, STO MOLTO BENE

A) BUONA SERA SIGNORA MARIA, COME STA?

B) BUONA SERA, IERI ERO UN PO' STANCE MA OGGI SONO IN GRAN FORMA

A) SALVE ALESSANDRO, COME VA?

B) TUTTO BENE, GRAZIE, E TE?

A) COSÌ COSÌ :   IERI ERO MALATO, MA ORA STO MEGLIO.

Chapter 6
Articles

The definite article (L'ARTICOLO DETERMINATIVO)

In English there is only one definite article: "the", while in the Italian language there are different forms, according to gender, number, and the first letter of the noun or adjective it precedes. You need to repet the article before each noun. You can see all of them in the table below.

Definite articles	Masculine	Feminine	English
Singular	IL LO* / L'**	LA / L'**	the
Plural	I GLI*	LE	the

* Only when the following word starts with *z, x, s + consonant, ps, pn, gn, i + vowel*
** Only when the following word (masculine or feminine) starts with a vowel (except i + vowel)
***   Only when the following word is feminine and starts with a vowel (except i + vowel)

The indefinite article (L'ARTICOLO INDETERMINATIVO)

The indefinite article corresponds to English "a/an" and is used with singular nouns. It also corresponds to the number 1.

Indefinite articles	Masculine	Feminine	English
Singular	UN UNO*	UNA UN'***	a / an

* Only when the following word starts with *z, x, s + consonant, ps, pn, gn, i + vowel*
** Only when the following word (masculine or feminine) starts with a vowel (except i + vowel)

*** Only when the following word is feminine and starts with a vowel (except i + vowel)

The partitive article (L'ARTICOLO PARTITIVO)

The partitive article is used to talk about imprecise or approximate quantities. You can use it both before singular nouns (DEL CAFFÈ, DEL LATTE) and before plural nouns of an unspecified amount (DEI RAGAZZI, DELLE FOTO, DEGLI ALBERI). The partitive is expressed in Italian by the preposition DI combined with the definite article. The preposition DI changes in DE when combined with the article, and you need to double the letter L when needed, as you can see in the table below:

Partitive articles	Masculine	Feminine	English
Singular	DEL (DI + IL) DELLO* (DI + LO)	DELLA (DI + LA)	some
Plural	DEI (DI + I) DEGLI* (DI + GLI)	DELLE	some

* Only when the following word starts with *z, x, s + consonant, ps, pn, gn, i + vowel*
** Only when the following word (masculine or feminine) starts with a vowel (except i + vowel)
*** Only when the following word is feminine and starts with a vowel (except i + vowel)

Test Your Italian!

1) Complete the text choosing among definite, indefinite and partitive articles.

CONOSCO ……. BAMBINO DI NOME PAOLO. ……. BAMBINO HA ……. FRATELLO PICCOLO CHE NON SA USARE ……. BICICLETTA. ……. GIORNO PAOLO CHIAMA ……. FRATELLO E GLI DA ……. CONSIGLI. TUTTI ……. GIORNI ……. FRATELLO DI PAOLO SI ALLENA, E ……. SETTIMANA DOPO RIESCE A PEDALARE BENE COME PAOLO.

2) Write the partitive article for each clause

1. ALCUNI ALBERI =
2. ALCUNI FRATELLI =
3. ALCUNE AMICHE =
4. ALCUNI CANI =
5. ALCUNE STORIE =

3) Write a sentence with each partitive article and noun of exercise no 2), e.g.: VEDO DEGLI ALBERI.

Answers

Exercise 1

CONOSCO UN BAMBINO DI NOME PAOLO. IL BAMBINO HA UN FRATELLO PICCOLO CHE NON SA USARE LA BICICLETTA. UN GIORNO PAOLO CHIAMA IL FRATELLO E GLI DA DEI CONSIGLI. TUTTI I GIORNI IL FRATELLO DI PAOLO SI ALLENA, E LA SETTIMANA DOPO RIESCE A PEDALARE BENE COME PAOLO.

Exercise 2

1. ALCUNI ALBERI = DEGLI ALBERI
2. ALCUNI FRATELLI = DEI FRATELLI
3. ALCUNE AMICHE = DELLE AMICHE
4. ALCUNI CANI = DEI CANI
5. ALCUNE STORIE = DELLE STORIE

Chapter 7: Colours

VIOLA **BLU** CELESTE VERDE CHIARO `GIALLO` ARANCIONE **ROSSO**
`BIANCO` **NERO** **MARRONE** **VERDE** **SCURO** ROSA GRIGIO

1) Write a sentence saying the color of each object:

LA MELA È ....

IL SOLE.......   ....

LA ....È ....

IL .... E IL ....

LA ……. È …………………………

LA ………………   ……………   ……………

LA …………. È ………….

IL ....

LE ....

IL ....

Answers

Exercise 1

LA MELA   È ROSSA

IL SOLE   È GIALLO

IL CIELO E IL MARE SONO BLU

LA ZUCCA   È ARANCIONE

LA PANTERA   È ROSA

IL BRUCO   È VERDE

LA FARFALLA   È VIOLA

LA FORMICA   È NERA

LE CASTAGNE SONO MARRONI

IL FIOCCO   È CELESTE

Chapter 8
Adjectives

In the Italian language there are male and female nouns; therefore the adjectives can be masculine or feminine. The general rule is that male nouns ends with letter "o", when they are singular, and with letter "i" when they are plural; in these cases they are <u>followed</u> by an adjective ending with letter "o" (if singular) or "i" (if plural). Female nouns ends with letter "a" when they are singular, and with "e" when they are plural, and they are <u>followed</u> by an adjective ending with letter "a" (if singular) or "e" (if plural).

1) Write the correct suffix in each sentence.

IL BAMBIN.:.   È CONTENT....

I BAMBIN... SONO CONTENT...

LA BAMBIN...   È CONTENT...

LE BAMBIN...   SONO CONTENT...

Now you can learn some of the most important adjectives in the Italian language:

ALTO	tall / high
BASSO	short
BUONO	good
CATTIVO	bad
SIMPATICO	friendly
GENTILE	gentle

GRANDE	big
PICCOLO	small
LARGO	large
STRETTO	narrow
LENTO	slow
VELOCE	fast
FORTE	strong
DEBOLE	weak
POVERO	poor
RICCO	rich
PULITO	clean
SPORCO	dirty
PUNTUALE	punctual
RITARDATARIO	latecoming
GRASSO	fat
MAGRO	thin

2) Link the adjectives to the appropriate person

BELLA
BRUTTO
ALTA
ANZIANO
BASSO
BIONDA
GRASSO
MAGRA
CALVO / PELATO
LISCIA
SPORTIVA
BAFFUTO

3) Write a sentence for each adjective taken from the list above:

1) L'UOMO È BRUTTO, ANZIANO, BASSO, GRASSO, CALVO / PELATO E BAFFUTO.
2) LA DONNA   È BELLA, ALTA, BIONDA, MAGRA, LISCIA E SPORTIVA
3) ....,..
4) ....
5) ....
6)   ....
7)   ....

8) ....

9) ....

10) ....

8.1 More or less? (PIÙ O MENO)

The Italian comparative and superlative cannot be created, as in English, by adding a suffix; this way is only used for the irregular adjectives. The only way to create comparatives and superlatives of regular adjectives (and adverbs) is to add modifiers like PIÙ and MENO (equivalent to "more" and "less").

8.1.1 Comparatives

The general rule, thus, is:

... PIÙ / MENO + ADJECTIVE / ADVERB + DI ...

Examples:

Adjectives

BART È PIÙ FELICE DI ABRAHAM
ABRAHAM È MENO FELICE DI BART

BART È PIÙ GIOVANE DI ABRAHAM
ABRAHAM È MENO GIOVANE DI BART

ABRAHAM È PIÙ ALTO DI BART
BART È MENO ALTO DI ABRAHAM

BART CORRE PIÙ VELOCEMENTE DI A.
A. CORRE MENO VELOCE DI BART

A. PARLA PIÙ LENTAMENTE DI BART
BART PARLA MENO LENTAMENTE DI ABRAHAM

→ COMPARATIVO DI UGUAGLIANZA: you use it when a quality is the same one in two people or objects. In Italian you can express it in this way:

... ADJECTIVE / ADVERB + COME ...

Examples:

BART È GIALLO COME ABRAHAM
ABRAHAM PARLA COME BART

8.1.2 Superlatives

In Italian, there are two forms of superlatives: the SUPERLATIVO RELATIVO (comparative) and the SUPERLATIVO ASSOLUTO (absolute).

→ The SUPERLATIVO RELATIVO represents a general quality that is expressed at its highest level, but it is still compared with that of other objects or

persons (more than 2). It is formed by using PIÙ or MENO between the determinative article and the adjective.
The general rule, thus, is:

... IL / LA / I / LE + PIÙ / MENO + ADJECTIVE + DI / TRA ...

Examples:

MAGGIE È LA PIÙ PICCOLA DELLA FAMIGLIA
LISA È LA PIÙ STUDIOSA TRA I BAMBINI
BART È IL MENO OBBEDIENTE DELLA FAMIGLIA

→ The SUPERLATIVO ASSOLUTO represents a general quality at its maximum level (like the elative). Normally, it is formed by adding the suffix -ISSIMO to the adjective's ending. The end of the suffix indicates the gender and number of the noun it refers to, therefore:
The general rule, thus, is:

... ADJECTIVE / ADVERB + -ISSIM + -O / A/ I / E

Examples:

MAGGIE È PICCOLISSIMA   (adjective)
LISA   È STUDIOSISSIMA   (adjective)
BART È DISOBBEDIENTISSIMO   (adjective)
OMER MANGIA VELOCISSIMO   (adverb)

Irregular forms

There are some adjectives and adverbs that have their own form of SUPERLATIVO and COMPARATIVO DI MAGGIORANZA (comparative using only PIÙ, and not MENO):

Positive		Comparative	Absolute superlative
BUONO	good	MIGLIORE (adj) better*	OTTIMO best
CATTIVO	bad	PEGGIORE (adj) worse*	PESSIMO worst

GRANDE big	MAGGIORE bigger	MASSIMO biggest
PICCOLO small	MINORE smaller	MINIMO smallest
BENE (adv) well	MEGLIO (adv) better*	BENISSIMO (adv) very well
MALE (adv) badly	PEGGIO (adv) worse*	MALISSIMO (adv) very badly

*Note: do not confuse MIGLIORE and PEGGIORE with MEGLIO and PEGGIO even though both are translated as "better" and "worse" in English. An easy way to remember which one is the adverb and which is the adjective, is to pay attention to the syllables: ME-GLIO and PEG-GIO have 2 syllables as does the word "ad-verb", so MEGLIO and PEGGIO are adverbs!

MI-GLIO-RE and PEG-GIO-RE have 3 syllables as does the word "ad-jec-tive", so MIGLIORE and PEGGIORE are adjectives!

E.g.:

VALENTINA SUONA IL PIANOFORTE MEGLIO DI TE. (adverb)
I SUOI STUDENTI SONO I MIGLIORI DELL'UNIVERSITÀ. (adjective).

4) Complete the sentences with the right words, to create comparatives, or superalatives of the two kinds. (The adjectives given in brackets are in the neutral form: masculine, singular)

1. IL MIO CANE HA LA CODA .... LUNGA .... TUO
2. TOMMASO È .... GIOVANE .... MARTINA
3. MICHELE SALTA .... IN ALTO .... TUTTI
4. LA SUA MACCHINA È .... (VELOCE – SUP. ASSOLUTO)
5. I TUOI NONNI SONO .... TUTTI (DOLCI – sup. relativo)
6. MATTEO È IL MIO FRATELLO .... (PIÙ PICCOLO)

7. SILVIA È LA MIA SORELLA ....(PIÙ GRANDE)
8. LUCIA   È ....   CHIARA   (FURBO – comp. uguaglianza)
9. RICCARDO OGGI SI SENTE .... (MALE – SUP. ASSOLUTO)
10. IERI AVEVO LA FEBBRE MA OGGI STO MOLTO .... (PIÙ BENE)
11. QUESTE LASAGNE SONO DAVVERO .... (BUONO – sup. assoluto)
12. QUESTO LIBRO È .... DELL'ALTRO (INTERESSANTE – comp. di minoranza)
13. L'EMILIA ROMAGNA   NON È .... LA TOSCANA (BELLO – comp. uguaglianza)

5) Underline comparatives and superlatives in the following article.

IN ITALIA NASCONO MOLTI MENO BAMBINI CHE IN ALTRI PAESI DEL MONDO. QUESTO È DOVUTO AL FATTO CHE LE PERSONE SI SPOSANO TARDISSIMO. UN'ALTRA CAUSA STA NEL FATTO CHE, RISPETTO AI PAESI PIÙ RICCHI, IN ITALIA DIVENTA UN PROBLEMA CRESCERE UN FIGLIO, PERCHÈ CI SONO MENO LAVORO E PIÙ ESIGENZE CHE IN ALTRI PAESI. L'ECONOMIA ITALIANA, IN QUESTO MOMENTO, È PEGGIORE DI QUELLA TEDESCA, MA ANCHE IN GERMANIA IL NUMERO DI NEONATI NON È TROPPO SUPERIORE A QUELLO ITALIANO.

6) Choose the correct word and write it in the sentence

1. QUESTA TORTA È ....
BUONISSIMA   MENO BUONISSIMA   PIÙ BUONISSIMA

2. QUESTA MACCHINA È   .... MIA
VELOCISSIMA   PIÙ VELOCE DELLA   LA PIÙ VELOCE DI

3. IL MIO COMPITO È .... TUO
PIÙ MEGLIO   MIGLIORE DEL   MEGLISSIMO DEL

4. MIA MADRE È .... DELLA FAMIGLIA
PIÙ BASSA   LA PIÙ BASSA   MINORE

5. STEFANO È .... MICHELE

ALTO COME   PIÙ ALTO   MENO ALTO

Answers

Exercise 1

IL BAMBINO   È CONTENTO; I BAMBINI SONO CONTENTI; LA BAMBINA È CONTENTA; LE BAMBINE   SONO CONTENTE

Exercise 3

L'UOMO È BRUTTO.
LA DONNA È BELLA.
LA DONNA È ALTA.
L'UOMO È ANZIANO.
L'UOMO È BASSO.
LA DONNA È BIONDA.
L'UOMO È GRASSO.
LA DONNA È MAGRA.
LA DONNA È LISCIA.
L'UOMO È CALVO / PELATO.
LA DONNA È SPORTIVA.
L'UOMO È BAFFUTO.

Exercise 4

1. IL MIO CANE HA LA CODA PIÙ LUNGA DEL TUO
2. TOMMASO È PIÙ GIOVANE DI MARTINA
3. MICHELE SALTA PIÙ IN ALTO DI TUTTI
4. LA SUA MACCHINA È VELOCISSIMA
5. I TUOI NONNI SONO I   PIÙ   DOLCI   DI   TUTTI
6. MATTEO È IL MIO FRATELLO MINORE
7. SILVIA È LA MIA SORELLA MAGGIORE
8. LUCIA   È FURBA COME CHIARA
9. RICCARDO OGGI SI SENTE MALISSIMO
10. IERI AVEVO LA FEBBRE MA OGGI STO MOLTO MEGLIO

11. QUESTE LASAGNE SONO DAVVERO OTTIME
12. QUESTO LIBRO È MENO INTERESSANTE DELL'ALTRO
13. L'EMILIA ROMAGNA   NON È BELLA COME LA TOSCANA

Exercise 5

IN ITALIA NASCONO MOLTI <u>MENO</u> BAMBINI <u>CHE</u> IN ALTRI PAESI DEL MONDO. QUESTO È DOVUTO AL FATTO CHE LE PERSONE SI SPOSANO <u>TARDISSIMO</u>. UN'ALTRA CAUSA STA NEL FATTO CHE, RISPETTO AI PAESI <u>PIÙ RICCHI</u>, IN ITALIA DIVENTA UN PROBLEMA CRESCERE UN FIGLIO, PERCHÈ CI SONO <u>MENO</u> LAVORO E <u>PIÙ</u> ESIGENZE CHE IN ALTRI PAESI. L'ECONOMIA ITALIANA, IN QUESTO MOMENTO, <u>È PEGGIORE</u> DI QUELLA TEDESCA, MA ANCHE IN GERMANIA IL NUMERO DI NEONATI NON <u>È</u> TROPPO <u>SUPERIORE</u> A QUELLO ITALIANO.

Exercise 6

1. QUESTA TORTA È BUONISSIMA
2. QUESTA MACCHINA È   PIÙ VELOCE DELLA MIA
3. IL MIO COMPITO È MIGLIORE DEL TUO
4. MIA MADRE È LA PIÙ BASSA DELLA FAMIGLIA
5. STEFANO È ALTO COME MICHELE

Chapter 9
The Verb "To Have" to Tell Your Age

IO	HO
TU	HAI
LUI / LEI	HA
NOI	ABBIAMO
VOI	AVETE
LORO	HANNO

I introduce myself:

In order to say your age in Italian, you have to use the verb "to have", AVERE, instead of the verb "to be" ESSERE. Italians feel the age as the number of years that they have lived, and so that they are "collecting", e.g.: I am 50 years old → IO HO 50 ANNI.

1) True or false? Read the introductions that the following characters have written about themselves, and decide if the following sentences are true (VERO) or false (FALSO).

 BUONGIORNO, IO SONO IL DOTTOR ROSSI.
HO 35 ANNI E ABITO A MILANO.   SONO ALTO, MAGRO, HO I CAPELLI CHIARI E GLI OCCHI SCURI. PORTO GLI OCCHIALI PERCHÉ SONO MIOPE. MI PIACE MOLTO IL MIO LAVORO.

CIAO A TUTTI, IO SONO LUCA E VENGO DA ROMA.
HO 18 ANNI E MI PIACE SUONARE LA CHITARRA.
SONO IL CHITARRISTA PIÙ BRAVO DELLA CITTÀ E HO MOLTI FAN.

CIAO, NOI SIAMO MARCO E LAURA E ABITIAMO IN TOSCANA. SIAMO FIDANZATI DA UN MESE. IO SONO BIONDA E HO GLI OCCHI AZZURRI, MENTRE LUI È CASTANO E HA GLI OCCHI VERDI. ABBIAMO ENTRAMBI 14 ANNI E ANDIAMO ALLA STESSA SCUOLA. SIAMO ALTI, MAGRI, E BELLI.

A) IL SIGNOR ROSSI È UN INFERMIERE

V   F

B) IL DOTTOR   ROSSI VIENE DAL SUD ITALIA

V   F

C) IL SIGNOR ROSSI HA I CAPELLI BIONDI E GLI OCCHI MARRONE SCURO V

F

D) IL SIGNOR ROSSI È CIECO

V   F

E) AL DOTTOR ROSSI NON PIACE MOLTO LAVORARE

V   F

F) LUCA VIENE DALLA CAPITALE ITALIANA

V   F

G) LUCA È MAGGIORENNE

V   F

H) A LUCA PIACE SUONARE, MA NON LO CONOSCE NESSUNO

     V   F

I) MARCO E LAURA ABITANO NELL'ITALIA CENTRALE

     V   F

L)   MARCO E LAURA SONO FRATELLI

         V   F

M)   MARCO E LAURA SONO COETANEI

     V   F

N) LAURA HA I CAPELLI E GLI OCCHI CHIARI   V

     F

O) MARCO HA I CAPELLI NERI E GLI OCCHI AZZURRI   V

     F

P)   MARCO E LAURA SONO DEI BEI RAGAZZI

     V   F

Q)   MARCO E LAURA LAVORANO IN UN RISTORANTE

     V   F

2) Now write the correct answer for the false sentences.

3) Describe yourself saying:

1) your name
2) your age
3) your physical description
4) where you live
5) what you like to do

Answers

Exercise 1

A) IL SIGNOR ROSSI È UN INFERMIERE

F

B) IL DOTTOR   ROSSI VIENE DAL SUD ITALIA

F

C) IL SIGNOR ROSSI HA I CAPELLI BIONDI E GLI OCCHI MARRONE SCURO V

D) IL SIGNOR ROSSI È CIECO

F

E) AL DOTTOR ROSSI NON PIACE MOLTO LAVORARE

F

F) LUCA VIENE DALLA CAPITALE ITALIANA

V

G) LUCA È MAGGIORENNE

V

H) A LUCA PIACE SUONARE, MA NON LO CONOSCE NESSUNO

F

I) MARCO E LAURA ABITANO NELL'ITALIA CENTRALE

V

L)   MARCO E LAURA SONO FRATELLI

F

M)   MARCO E LAURA SONO COETANEI

V

N) LAURA HA I CAPELLI E GLI OCCHI CHIARI   V

O) MARCO HA I CAPELLI NERI E GLI OCCHI AZZURRI

F

P)   MARCO E LAURA SONO DEI BEI RAGAZZI

   V

Q)   MARCO E LAURA LAVORANO IN UN RISTORANTE

   F

Exercise 2

A) IL SIGNOR ROSSI È UN DOTTORE

B) IL DOTTOR   ROSSI VIENE DAL NORD ITALIA (MILANO)

D) IL SIGNOR ROSSI È MIOPE

E) AL DOTTOR ROSSI PIACE MOLTO LAVORARE

H) A LUCA PIACE SUONARE, E HA MOLTI FAN

L)   MARCO E LAURA SONO FIDANZATI

O) MARCO HA I CAPELLI CASTANI (MARRONI) E GLI OCCHI VERDI

Q)   MARCO E LAURA VANNO A SCUOLA

Chapter 10
The Weather, The Months, And The Days of The Week

The typical topic when you talk to someone you don't know well is the weather, for this reason it may be very useful to know it well.

→ The four Italian seasons (STAGIONE / -I) are PRIMAVERA (Spring), ESTATE (Summer), AUTUNNO (Autumn) and INVERNO (Winter).

1) Read the dialog and guess which seasons the two ladies are talking about

A)   ....
♀) OGGI FA VERAMENTE MOLTO FREDDO. HO LE MANI E IL NASO CONGELATI. SEMBRA CHE OGNI TANTO VOGLIA SPUNTARE IL SOLE, MA LA TEMPERATURA È TROPPO BASSA PER RISCALDARMI.
♂) È VERO, E POI C' È UN VENTO FORTISSIMO! SPERIAMO ARRIVI PRESTO LA PRIMAVERA.

B)   ....
♀) CHE CALDO! CI SARANNO ALMENO 30° ALL'OMBRA!
♂) SI, MA LA COSA PEGGIORE È TUTTA QUESTA UMIDITÀ: RENDE IL CALDO ANCORA PIÙ INSOPPORTABILE.
♀) GIÀ, MA MENO MALE CHE OGNI TANTO QUALCHE NUVOLETTA COPRE UN PO' IL SOLE.

C)   ....
♀) OGGI SI STA PROPRIO BENE! CI SONO UNA LEGGERA BREZZA RINFRESCANTE E UN BEL SOLE. MI PIACE TANTO QUESTO PERIODO DELL'ANNO: È PERFETTO PER STARE ALL'ARIA APERTA.
♂) HAI RAGIONE, ED È BELLO VEDERE DI NUOVO GLI ALBERI E I PRATI FIORITI.

D)   ....
♀) CREDO CHE OGGI SIA UNO DEGLI ULTIMI GIORNI DI BEL TEMPO. LA TEMPERATURA È PIACEVOLE, MA SI SENTE CHE STA RINFRESCANDO. HO PAURA CHE PRESTO ARRIVERANNO IL FREDDO E LA PIOGGIA.

♂) A ME NON DISPIACE QUESTA STAGIONE: ALMENO NON FA PIÙ CALDO COME PRIMA E NON CI SONO ZANZARE! IN PIÙ TROVO MOLTO BELLI GLI ALBERI SPOGLI E LE FOGLIE ARANCIONI A TERRA.

→ The months _ I MESI:
GENNAIO, FEBBRAIO, MARZO, APRILE, MAGGIO, GIUGNO, LUGLIO, AGOSTO, SETTEMBRE, OTTOBRE, NOVEMBRE, DICEMBRE.

2) Guess in which month these events happen, and link them to the write month:

A .... SI FA L'OLIO	GENNAIO
A .... VADO AL MARE	FEBBRAIO
A .... COMINCIA LA PRIMAVERA	MARZO
A .... FESTEGGIAMO IL NATALE.	APRILE
A .... FESTEGGIAMO LA PASQUA	MAGGIO
A .... VADO IN VACANZA	GIUGNO
A .... FA MOLTO CALDO	LUGLIO
A .... DEVO STUDIARE TANTO	AGOSTO
A .... FA MOLTO FREDDO	SETTEMBRE
A .... PIOVE PIÙ SPESSO	OTTOBRE
A .... SI RACCOGLIE L'UVA	NOVEMBRE
A .... FINISCONO LE VACANZE DI NATALE	DICEMBRE

→ The days of the week _ I GIORNI DELLA SETTIMANA.
LUNEDÌ, MARTEDÌ, MERCOLEDÌ, GIOVEDÌ, VENERDÌ, SABATO, DOMENICA
On Monday = **IL** LUNEDÌ

3) True or false? Read what Maria does during her week, and decide if the following sentences are true (VERO) or false (FALSO). Then correct the wrong sentences.

IL LUNEDÌ MI SVEGLIO PRESTO PERCHÉ DEVO ANDARE A FIRENZE. LAVORO LÌ TUTTA LA SETTIMANA E TORNO PER IL FINESETTIMANA.

IL MARTEDÌ MI SVEGLIO PIÙ TARDI, VADO A LAVORO E NELLA PAUSA PRANZO VADO IN PISCINA. LA SERA INCONTRO LA MIA AMICA FEDERICA E ANDIAMO A VEDERE UN FILM AL CINEMA.

IL MERCOLEDÌ LAVORO SOLO LA MATTINA, COSÌ IL POMERIGGIO POSSO ANDARE A FARE UN GIRO IN CENTRO: MI PIACE VEDERE LE VETRINE E FARE DEGLI ACQUISTI.

IL GIOVEDÌ LAVORO SIA MATTINA CHE POMERIGGIO, MA COME IL MARTEDÌ HO IL TEMPO DI ANDARE A FARE SPORT NELLA PAUSA PRANZO.

IL VENERDÌ MI SVEGLIO MOLTO FELICE PERCHÉ SO CHE È L'ULTIMO GIORNO DI LAVORO E NEL TARDO POMERIGGIO TORNO A CASA DALLA MIA FAMIGLIA.

IL SABATO MATTINA DORMO FINO ALLE 10. POI MI ALZO, FACCIO LA COLAZIONE E ESCO A FARE UNA PASSEGGIATA SUL MARE. PRANZO CON LA MIA FAMIGLIA E PER CENA VADO IN PIZZERIA CON GLI AMICI.

LA DOMENICA VADO IN CAMPAGNA DAI MIEI NONNI. LÌ INCONTRO TUTTI I MIEI PARENTI E STIAMO INSIEME TUTTO IL POMERIGGIO. LA SERA VADO A LETTO PRESTO PERCHÉ LA MATTINA DOPO RICOMINCIA LA SETTIMANA.

A) MARIA NON HA BISOGNO DELL'AUTO PER ANDARE A LAVORO   V
     F

B) MARIA HA IL LUNEDÌ DI FESTA
     V   F

C) IL MARTEDÌ MARIA PUÒ FARE SPORT
     V   F

D) A MARIA PIACE VEDERE I FILM
     V   F

E) IL MERCOLEDÌ POMERIGGIO, È UN GIORNO MOLTO IMPEGNATIVO
     V   F

F) MARIA VA IN PISCINA UNA VOLTA ALLA SETTIMANA
          V   F

G) IL VENERDÌ MARIA SI SVEGLIA FELICE PERCHÉ NON DEVE LAVORARE   V
          F

H) IL VENERDÌ MATTINA MARIA TORNA A CASA
          V   F

I) IL SABATO MATTINA MARIA FA COLAZIONE AL BAR CON GLI AMICI   V
          F

L)   IL SABATO MARIA NUOTA NEL MARE
          V   F

M)   MARIA TRASCORRE LA DOMANICA CON LA FAMIGLIA E I PARENTI   V
          F

N) LA DOMENICA SERA MARIA TORNA A FIRENZE
          V   F

4) Now it's your turn: write what you do!

IL LUNEDÌ ....

Answers

Exercise 1

A) INVERNO
B) ESTATE
C) PRIMAVERA
D) AUTUNNO

Exercise 2

A GENNAIO FINISCONO LE VACANZE DI NATALE
A FEBBRAIO FA MOLTO FREDDO

A MARZO COMINCIA LA PRIMAVERA
A APRILE FESTEGGIAMO LA PASQUA
A MAGGIO DEVO STUDIARE TANTO
A GIUGNO VADO AL MARE
A LUGLIO VADO IN VACANZA
A AGOSTO FA MOLTO CALDO
A SETTEMBRE SI RACCOGLIE L'UVA
A OTTOBRE PIOVE PIÙ SPESSO
A NOVEMBRE SI FA L'OLIO
A DICEMBRE FESTEGGIAMO IL NATALE.

Exercise 3

A) MARIA NON HA BISOGNO DELL'AUTO PER ANDARE A LAVORO
      F

B) MARIA HA IL LUNEDÌ DI FESTA
        F

C) IL MARTEDÌ MARIA PUÒ FARE SPORT
      V

D) A MARIA PIACE VEDERE I FILM
      V

E) IL MERCOLEDÌ POMERIGGIO, È UN GIORNO MOLTO IMPEGNATIVO
       F

F) MARIA VA IN PISCINA UNA VOLTA ALLA SETTIMANA
       F

G) IL VENERDÌ MARIA SI SVEGLIA FELICE PERCHÉ NON DEVE LAVORARE
      F

H) IL VENERDÌ MATTINA MARIA TORNA A CASA
       F

I) IL SABATO MATTINA MARIA FA COLAZIONE AL BAR CON GLI AMICI
      F

L)   IL SABATO MARIA NUOTA NEL MARE
       F

M)   MARIA TRASCORRE LA DOMANICA CON LA FAMIGLIA E I PARENTI   V

N) LA DOMENICA SERA MARIA TORNA A FIRENZE
       F

A) MARIA HA BISOGNO DELL'AUTO PER ANDARE A LAVORO, PERCHÉ LAVORA IN UN'ALTRA CITTÀ (A FIRENZE)

B) MARIA NON HA IL LUNEDÌ DI FESTA, MA LAVORA.

E) IL MERCOLEDÌ POMERIGGIO MARIA È LIBERA PERCHÉ NON LAVORA, QUINDI PUÒ DEDICARSI AGLI HOBBY

F) MARIA VA IN PISCINA DUE VOLTE ALLA SETTIMANA: IL MARTEDÌ E IL GIOVEDÌ.

G) IL VENERDÌ MARIA SI SVEGLIA FELICE PERCHÉ È L'ULTIMO GIORNO DI LAVORO E   LA SERA TORNA A CASA

H) MARIA TORNA A CASA IL VENERDÌ NEL TARDO POMERIGGIO

I) IL SABATO MATTINA MARIA FA COLAZIONE A CASA, E DOPO ESCE

L)   IL SABATO MARIA PASSEGGIA IN RIVA AL MARE

N) MARIA TORNA A FIRENZE IL LUNEDÌ MATTINA

Chapter 11: The clock (L'OROLOGIO)

SONO LE SETTE. (It is seven A.M.)
SONO LE DICIANNOVE (It is seven P.M.)

In Italy, as in most of Europe, people use the so-called "official time" in train schedules, radio, TV, performances, movie timetables and office hours. In informal situations Italians may use the numbers from 1 to 12 to indicate time, and the context of the conversation will usually be sufficient to understand if they mean "a.m." or "p.m.".   In the "official time" you just need to go on with the numbers, after 12, untill 24. It means that 1 p.m. is 13; 2   p.m. is 14; 11 p.m. is 23, and so on.

And what about midnight? Is it 00:00 or 24:00? Actually you may use both, even if they are slightly different: in the 24-hour time notation, the day begins at midnight, 00:00, and the last minute of the day begins at 23:59. Sometimes the notation 24:00 is also used to refer to midnight at the end of a given date, therefore 24:00 of one day is the same time as 00:00 of the following day. An example is given by the opening and closing offices hours, e.g. "00:00–24:00", "07:00–24:00". Other examples are some railway timetables that show 00:00 as departure time and 24:00 as arrival time, and legal contracts that often run from the start date at 00:00 till the end date at 24:00.

In the following table you can see some of the most useful questions, answers and terms related to telling time.

| CHE ORE SONO, PER FAVORE? | What time is it, please? |

CHE ORA È?	What time is it?
È* L'UNA.	It's one o'clock.
È MEZZOGIORNO.	It's noon.
È MEZZANOTTE.	It's midnight.
SONO* LE TRE E QUINDICI / SONO LE TRE E UN QUARTO.	It's three fifteen. It's a quarter past three
È MEZZOGIORNO E DIECI.	It's 12:10.
SONO LE DIECI E MEZZO	It's half past ten.
MATTINO	morning
POMERIGGIO	afternoon
SERA	evening
E UN QUARTO	a quarter past
E MEZZO	half past
UN QUARTO A / MENO UN QUARTO	a quarter to a quarter to
IN PUNTO	sharp

*Note that if the time is "one o'clock", "noon", or "midnight", the verb of the answer is in the singular form (È) ; for all other times, it is plural (SONO).

The following table shows how you should tell the time from 2:00 to 3:00.

02.00	Sono le due.
02.05	Sono le due e cinque.
02.10	Sono le due e dieci.
02.15	Sono le due e un quarto.
02.20	Sono le due e venti.
02.30	Sono le due e mezzo.
02.40	Manca venti alle tre / Sono le tre meno venti.

02.45	Manca un quarto alle tre / Sono le tre meno un quarto.
02.50	Manca dieci alle tre / Sono le tre meno dieci.
03.00	Sono le tre.

1) Write down for each clock what time it is, in the two ways ("a.m." and

"p.m.")

A) ....

A) ....

B) ....

B) ....

C) ....

C) ....

D).......................................
D).......................................

E).......................................
E).......................................

F).......................................
F).......................................

2) Translate the following times:

- It's a quarter to three   ....
- It's a   quarter past ten   ....
- It's half past two   ....
- It's midnight   ....

- It's eleven o'clock ....
- It's five past eight ....

Some adverbs of time

AVVERBI TI TEMPO	Adverbs of time
ORA / ADESSO	Now
OGGI	Today
IERI	Yesterday
IERI L'ALTRO / L'ALTRO IERI	The day before yesterday
DOMANI	Tomorrow
DOMANI L'ALTRO / DOPODOMANI	The day after tomorrow
PRIMA	Before / first
POI	Then
DOPO	After
SEMPRE	Always
SPESSO	Often
DI SOLITO	Usually
MAI*	Never
QUASI MAI	Hardly ever
TARDI	Late
PRESTO	Early / soon
SUBITO	Immediately
GIÀ	Already
ANCORA	Yet / still
PRIMA O POI	Sooner or later
ADESSO O MAI PIÙ	Now or never

The adverb MAI is always used after the verb introduced by the negation adverb NON: in Italy two negations do not affirm! E.g.: I have <u>never</u> seen that film → <u>NON</u> HO <u>MAI</u> VISTO QUEL FILM.

3) Complete the timeline with the appropriate time adverbs.

```
    *_____*_____*_____*_____
_____*>
.....................                    .........................                    OGGI
    ...........................                    .......................
```

4) Translate the following dialogs with the appropriate time adverbs

1. A) VUOI UN PIATTO DI PASTA? (Would you like some pasta?)

B) NO GRAZIE, HO .... MANGIATO. (No thanks, I have already eaten)

2. (Yesterday I couldn't go to the cinema) .... NON SONO POTUTA ANDARE AL CINEMA, (but today I want to go there) MA ....CI VAGLIO ANDARE.

3. MI DISPAICE, MA .... DEVO USCIRE (I'm sorry, but now I have to go out)

4. NON SEI .... PRONTA? (Aren't you ready yet?)

5. .... DEVO FARE I COMPITI, ... POSSO USCIRE. (First I have to do my homework, then I can go out)

6. NOI ANDIAMO .... A TEATRO. (We often go to the theatre)

7. LUCA È .... IN RITARDO. (Luca is always late)

8. .... O .... VOGLIO ANDARE IN AMERICA (Sooner or later I want to go to America)

9. LORO NON USANO .... LA MACCHINA. (They never use their car)

10. NON ANDIAMO .... A SCIARE. (We hardly ever go skiing)

Answers
Chapter 11 Exercise 1

A) È l'una e cinquantadue
A) Mancano otto minuti alle due
A) Sono le tredici e cinquantadue

B) Sono le tre e trenta
B) Sono le tre e mezzo
B) Sono le quindici e trenta

C) Sono le sette e ventidue
C) Sono le diciannove e ventidue

D) Sono le tre e trentacinque
D) Mancano venticinque minuti alle quattro
D) Sono le quindici e trentacinque

E) Sono le otto e tre (minuti)
E) Sono le venti e tre (minuti)

F) Sono le dieci e quindici
F) Sono le dieci e un quarto
F) Sono le ventidue e quindici

Chapter 11 Exercise 2

- It's a quarter to three   Manca un quarto alle tre
- It's a quarter past ten   Sono le dieci e un quarto
- It's half past two   Sono le due e mezzo
- It's midnight   È mezzanotte
- It's eleven o'clock   Sono le undici
- It's five past eight   Sono le otto e cinque

Chapter 11 Exercise 3

```
      *_____*_____*_____*_____
_____*>
Ieri l'altro                    ieri                                    OGGI
        domani          domani l'altro
```

Chapter 11 Exercise 4

11. a) vuoi un piatto di pasta?
    b) no grazie, ho GIÀ mangiato.
12. IERI non sono potuta andare al cinema,   ma OGGI ci vaglio andare.
13. mi dispaice, ma ADESSO / ORA devo uscire
14. non sei ANCORA pronta?
15. PRIMA devo fare i compiti, POI posso uscire.
16. noi andiamo SPESSO a teatro.
17. luca è SEMPRE in ritardo.
18. PRIMA o POI voglio andare in America
19. loro non usano MAI la macchina.
20. non andiamo QUASI MAI a sciare.

Chapter 12
Asking Questions: Who, What, When, Where, Why, How, How Much

Italian interrogative adverbs (AVVERBI INTERROGATIVI) introduce a question that relates to manner, place, time, size or value and reason.

They are used both in direct questions: DOVE VAI? (where are you going?) and in indirect questions DIMMI DOVE VAI (tell me where you are going).

En. adverb	It. adverb	Italian example	English translation
Who	CHI	CHI SEI?	Who are you?
What	(CHE) COSA	COSA FAI?	What are you doing?
When	QUANDO	QUANDO SEI NATO?	When were you born?
Where	DOVE	DOVE VIVI?	Where do you live?
Why*	PERCHÉ COME MAI	PERCHÉ STUDI L'ITALIANO? COME MAI STUDI L'ITALIANO?	Why are you studying Italian?
How	COME	COME STAI?	How are you?
Which	QUALE	QUALE PREFERISCI?	Which one do you prefer?
How much	QUANTO	QUANTO COSTA?	How much does it cost?
How many**	QUANTI	QUANTI ANNI HAI?	How old are you?*

* In Italian you can use PERCHÉ in both questions and answers, so it is different from the English where you must use "why" in questions and "because" in answers. There is an adverb that corresponds a little bit to the English "because": POICHÉ; so you could use POICHÉ, answering to a question, but it is less common, and more formal.

**Note: remember that in order to say your age, Italians use the verb "to have", and the interrogative adverb is QUANTI (how many): something that sound in English like *how many years do you have? For this reason you may have heard Italian people saying I have (instead of I am) 20 years old.

1) Complete the sentences with the correct adverb.
1. .... COSTA UN CHILO DI MELE?
2. .... VIENE CON ME AL CINAME?
3. .... NON SEI VENUTO A SCUOLA IERI?
4. .... VAI IN VACANZA QUEST'ESTATE?
5. .... ANNI HA TUO FRATELLO?
6. .... FETSEGGI IL TUO COMPLEANNO?
7. CON .... PREFERISCI GIOCARE?
8. .... SPORT PREFERISCI?
9. .... HAI MANGIATO A PRANZO?
10. .... STA LA TUA NONNA?

Answers

Chapter 12, Exercise 1

1) QUANTO
2) CHI
3) PERCHÉ / COME MAI
4) DOVE
5) QUANTI
6)   QUANDO
7)   CHI
8) QUALE / CHE
9)   COSA
10) COME

Chapter 13
Modal Verbs (VERBI MODALI)

OGGI **VOGLIO** FARE QUALCOSA DI DIVERSO: OGNI GIORNO **DEVO** ALZARMI PRESTO PER LAVORARE MOLTO, MA OGGI È FESTA E **POSSO** ANDARE AL MARE CON I MIEI AMICI.

(Today I **want** to do something different: every day I **have to** wake up early and to work a lot, but today it is holiday and I **can** go to the beach with my friends)

	DOVERE	POTERE	VOLERE
IO	DEVO	POSSO	VOGLIO
TU	DEVI	PUOI	VUOI
LUI / LEI	DEVE	PUÒ	VUOLE
NOI	DOBBIAMO	POSSIAMO	VOGLIAMO
VOI	DOVETE	POTETE	VOLETE
LORO	DEVONO	POSSONO	VOGLIONO

These verbs are auxiliary verbs and must be followed by the infinitive, without any preposition:
DOVERE / POTERE / VOLERE + infinitive.

Note: To say that you are able to do something, Italians don't use the verb "POTERE", but "SAPERE" (SAPERE means both to "to be able to" and to "to know"):

I can speak German → IO SO PARLARE TEDESCO.

The verb POTERE is used to ask for permission and to say that you have the possibility of doing something:

SARA PUÒ COMPRARSI UNA CASA: HA MOLTI SOLDI! (Sara can buy a house: she has got a lot of money!)

POSSO FARTI UNA DOMANDA? (Can / may I ask you a question?)

1) POTERE or SAPERE? Write the correct verb in the right form.
1. SONO IN RIUNIONE, NON .... PARLARE.
2. LUCA LAVORA IN RUSSIA MA NON .... UNA PAROLA DI RUSSO.
3. OGGI NON.............VENIRE IN CENTRO PERCHÉ HO DA FARE.
4. (LEI) SCUSI, ... CHE ORE SONO?
5. (VOI)..................... VENIRE A CASA MIA OGGI? VOGLIO FARVI VEDERE LA
MIA NUOVA CASA.
6. (TU)............. SCIARE?
7. MIA FIGLIA NON.............VENIRE IN BARCA CON VOI, NON ....
NUOTARE.
8. (VOI) .... GIOCARE A PALLAVOLO ?
9. (NOI) NON .... DOVE ABITA LUCIA.
10. SE NON HANNO LA MACCHINA .... PRENDERE IL TRENO.

2) Write the sentences using the suggested words

    1. IO DOVERE PARTIRE DOMANI MA VOLERE PARTIRE OGGI
IO ....
    2. IO DOVERE LAVORARE MA VOLERE ANDARE AL CINEMA
IO ....
    3. LEI POTERE USCIRE MA VOLERE RESTARE CON ME
LEI ....
    4. NOI VOLERE ANDARE IN MONTAGNA MA NON SAPERE SCIARE
....
    5. TU DOVERE ASCOLARE QUELLO CHE (IO) DIRE
....

Answers

Chapter 13 Exercise 1

1) POSSO
2) SA
3) POSSO
4) POTETE
5) SA

6) SAI
7) PUÒ – SA
8) SAPETE
9) SO
10) POSSONO

Chapter 13 Exercise 2

1. IO DEVO PARTIRE DOMANI MA VOGLIO PARTIRE OGGI
2. IO DEVO LAVORARE MA VOGLIO ANDARE AL CINEMA
3. LEI PUÒ USCIRE MA VUOLE RESTARE CON ME
4. NOI VOGLIAMO ANDARE IN MONTAGNA MA NON SAPPIAMO SCIARE
5. TU DEVI ASCOLARE QUELLO CHE DICO

Chapter 14: Reflexive Verbs (VERBI RIFLESSIVI)

In the Italian language there are some reflexive verbs: in these cases the action carried out by the subject is performed on the same subject. The reflexive verbs don't end with -E (-AR-E), in the infinitive but with the pronoun -SI (-AR-SI). For example, LAVARE (to wash) becomes LAVARSI (to wash oneself) in the reflexive. -SI is an additional pronoun, known as the reflexive pronoun, which is needed when conjugating reflexive verbs. In the infinitive form it is attached to the end of the verb, while in the conjugated verbs it becomes a separate word, that occurs between the subject and the verb, and it needs to be conjugated as well:

IO	MI	LAVO
TU	TI	LAVI
LUI / LEI	SI	LAVA
NOI	CI	LAVIAMO
VOI	VI	LAVATE
LORO	SI	LAVANO

Note that some reflexive verbs can be used nonreflexively (without the reflexive pronouns). In this case, you need the direct object and their meaning changes a bit:

IO	/	LAVO	what?	IL PAVIMENTO (the floor)
TU	/	LAVI		
LUI / LEI	/	LAVA		
NOI	/	LAVIAMO		
VOI	/	LAVATE		
LORO	/	LAVANO		

TU **TI** ALZI.   (You get up.)
TU <u>ALZI</u> LA SEDIA.   (You lift the chair.)

If you use one of these verbs after a modal verb, you have to use the infinitive form, and in this case the reflexive pronoun needs to be attached to the verb, at the end of it:

IO	VOGLIO	LAVAR-MI

TU	VUOI	LAVAR-TI
LUI / LEI	VUOLE LAVAR-SI	
NOI	VOGLIAMO	LAVAR-CI
VOI	VOLETE	LAVAR-VI
LORO	VOGLIONO	LAVAR-SI

In this table you can see some of the most common reflexive verbs in Italian:

ADDORMENTARSI	To fall asleep
ALZARSI	To get up
ARRABBIARSI	To get angry
CHIAMARSI (io mi chiamo Michela)	To be named (My name is Michela)
DIVERTIRSI	To enjoy
FARSI (MALE)	To get hurt / To hurt oneself
FIDANZARSI	To get engaged
INNAMORARSI (DI)	To fall in love (with)
LAVARSI	To wash oneself
METTERSI (UN VESTITO)	To put (clothing) on
PETTINARSI	To comb one's hair
RADERSI / FARSI LA BARBA	To shave
SEDERSI	To sit down
SENTIRSI	To feel
SPOGLIARSI	To undress
SPOSARSI	To get married
SVEGLIARSI	To wake up
VESTIRSI	To get dressed

1) Translate the following sentences with some of these reflexive verbs.
   1. I get up early …………………………………………………………………..
   2. I fall in love, I get engaged and then I get married…………………………………………………….

3. I feel very well …………………………………………………………
4. In the morning I get dressed and in the evening I undress……………………………………………
5. I wake up at 7.00 but I get up at 7.30.

   …………………………………………………………
6. While I comb my hair, my husband shaves his beard

   …………………………………………………………
7. When she is late I get angry …………………………………………………………
8. Sometimes I can't fall asleep …………………………………………………………
9. I want to put on a beautfull dress

   …………………………………………………………
10. I don't want to get hurt …………………………………………………………

Chapter 14 Exercise 1

1) IO MI SVEGLIO PRESTO
2) MI INNAMORO, MI FIDANZO E POI MI SPOSO
3) MI SENTO MOLTO BENE
4) LA MATTINA MI VESTO E LA SERA MI SPOGLIO
5) IO MI SVEGLIO ALLE 7.00 MA MI ALZO ALLE 7.30
6) MENTRE IO MI PETTINO, MIO MARITO SI RASA / SI FA LA BARBA
7) QUANDO LEI RITARDA IO MI ARRABBIO
8) A VOLTE NON RIESCO AD ADDORMENTARMI
9) VOGLIO METTERMI UN BEL VESTITO
10) NON VOGLIO FARMI MALE

Chapter 15   Where Is It? (DOV'È?)

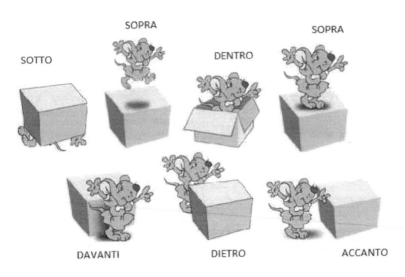

SOTTO   SOPRA   DENTRO   SOPRA

DAVANTI   DIETRO   ACCANTO

DI FRONTE

TRA

1) For each picture write where is the boy, the mouse or the dog.

....

....

....

....

....

....

....

....

....

There is – there are _ C'È – CI SONO

In Italian to state the existence or presence of something or someone you can use C'È (from CI È) and CI SONO, that correspond to the English "there is" and "there are".

In the following table you can see the Italian words of the most commons objects you find in a bedroom (CAMERA), with the English translation.

LETTO	Bed
ARMADIO	Wardrobe
TENDA	Curtain
TAPPETO	Carpet

COMODINO	Night table
LAMPADA	Lamp
SCRIVANIA	Desk
SEDIA	Chair
TELEVISIONE	Television
PIANTA	Plant
PORTA	Door
FINESTRA	Window
ACQUARIO	Fish tank
SVEGLIA	Alarm clock

2) Describe this bedroom, using the prepositions and the words that you have just learnt.

NELLA CAMERA C' È.......
NELLA CAMERA CI SONO.......

Answers

Chapter 15 Exercise 1

1) IL BAMBINO È SOPRA ALLO / LO SKATEBOARD
2) IL BAMBINO È DI FRONTE ALL'ORSACCHIOTTO
3) IL BAMBINO È DAVANTI ALL'ASINO
4) IL BAMBINO È DIETRO IL TAMBURO
5) IL BAMBINO È DENTRO IL CANOTTO

6) IL CANE È SOPRA LA SEDIA
7) IL BAMBINO È TRA I CESPUGLI
8) IL TOPO È DAVANTI AL FORMAGGIO
9) IL BAMBINO È SOTTO IL RAMO

Chapter 15 Exercise 2

NELLA CAMERA   C'È UN LETTO. SOPRA IL LETTO   C'È UNA LAMPADA.
ACANTO AL LETTO   C'È UN COMODINO. SOPRA IL COMODINO   C'È UNA
SVEGLIA. DAVANTI AL COMODINO   C'È UN TAPPETO. ACCANTO AL LETTO
C'È UNA PIANTA. ACCANTO ALLA PIANTA C'È LA PORTA. L'ACQUARIO È TRA
LA PORTA E L'ARMADIO. DI FRONTE AL LETTO   C'È UNA SCRIVANIA.
DAVANTI ALLA SCRIVANIA   C'È UNA SEDIA. SOPRA ALLA SCRIVANIA C'È UNA
TELEVISIONE

Chapter 16
Possessive Adjectives

Possessive adjectives indicate possession or ownership. They correspond to the English "my", "your", "his", "her", "its", "our" and "their". An important difference between the English and the Italian possessive adjectives is that the Italian ones are preceded by the definite articles: IL, LA, I and LE, that agree in gender and number with the noun possessed, not with the possessor.

Masculine singular	Feminine singular	Masculine plural	Feminine plural
IL MIO	LA MIA	I MIEI	LE MIE
IL TUO	LA TUA	I TUOI	LE TUE
IL SUO	LA SUA	I SUOI	LE SUE
IL NOSTRO	LA NOSTRA	I NOSTRI	LE NOSTRE
IL VOSTRO	LA VOSTRA	I VOSTRI	LE VOSTRE
IL LORO	LA LORO	I LORO	LE LORO

Note: there is an exception with the words MADRE (mother) and PADRE (father), because they are never preceded by both the article and the possessive adjective:
LA MADRE DI LUCA SI CHIAMA MARIA, SUO PADRE SI CHIAMA GIOVANNI.

1) Underline the correct answer

1. DOMANI IO E ……… MADRE ANDIAMO INSIEME IN CENTRO A FARE SHOPPING
MIA   LA SUA   I MIEI

2. COMPRO ……………… CELLULARE SOLO SE MI ASSICURI CHE FUNZIONA.
LE TUE   I TOUI   IL TUO

3.   PRENDO …………… NUMERO DI TELEFONO SE VOI SIETE D'ACCORDO
MIO   IL VOSTRO   LA SUA

4. TI PRESTO .... MACCHINA, SE .... È ROTTA.
LA MIA   IL MIO   LORO
TUA   LA TUA   IL TUO

5. PUOI DIRE A CHIARA CHE DOMANI PUOI PORTARE ANCHE
............................CANE?
NOSTRO   IL SUO   IL TUO

6. NOI POSSIAMO ANDARE AL CINEMA SOLO SE .... GENITORI CI
DANNO IL PERMESSO.
SUOI   I NOSTRI   LORO

7. AL DOTTOR ROSSI PIACE MOLTO .... LAVORO.
SUO   LA SUA   IL SUO

8. .... SORELLE SI CHIAMANO SILVIA E ELISA
I MIEI   LE MIE   LE LORO

9. ALCUNI CANTANTI SCRIVONO .... CANZONI
LA SUA   LE LORO   VOSTRE

10. .... AMICI ARRIVERANNO PRESTO
I MIEI   TUOI   VOSTRI

Answers

Chapter 16 Exercise 1

1. MIA
2. IL TUO
3. IL VOSTRO
4. LA MIA _ LA TUA
5. IL SUO
6. I NOSTRI
7. IL SUO
8. LE MIE
9. LE LORO

- I MIEI

Chapter 17
Demonstrative Adjectives

While in English you only have "this", "that", "these" and "those" in Italian you have to choose if the noun is masculine or feminine, and conjugate the adjective in the right form.

This	That	These	Those
QUESTO	QUELLO*	QUESTI	QUELLI
QUESTA	QUELLA	QUESTE	QUELLE
			QUEI
			QUEGLI*

* Only when the following word starts with *z, x, s + consonant, ps, pn, gn, i + vowel*

1) Complete the sentences with the right demonstrative adjective

A) .... LIBRO MI PIACE MOLTISSIMO

B) HAI VISTO COME È BELLA .... VILLA?

C) .... FINESETTIMANA VADO A SCIARE CON I MIEI AMICI

D) .... RAGAZZE SONO LE SORELLE DI PIETRO

E) NON SO SE SCEGLIERE .... QUA O .... LÀ

F) .... FIORI SONO MERAVIGLIOSI

G) MI PIACE DI PIÙ .... TORTA

H) .... ALBERI HANNO PIÙ DI CENTO ANNI

I) .... SONO GLI OCCHI PIÙ BELLI CHE IO ABBIA MAI VISTO

2) Translate the following sentences
1) This dog is called Bobby
2) That car is new
3) Those trees are very big
4) Those flowers are sunflowers
5) These ladies are very kind

Answers
Chapter 17 Exercise 1

A) QUESTO

B) QUELLA
C) QUESTO
D) QUELLE
E) QUESTO _ QUELLO
F) QUESTI
G) QUESTA
H) QUEGLI

Chapter 17 Exercise 2

1. QUESTO CANE SI CHIAMA BOBBY
2. QUESTA MACCHINA è NUOVA
3. QUEGLI ALBERI SONO MOLTO GRANDI
4. QUEI FIORI SONO GIRASOLI
5. QUESTE SIGNORE SONO MOLTO GENTILI

Chapter 18
I like it! (MI PIACE)

To say that you like something, in Italian, you have to use a different structure:

a) I (Who? subject)   like (verb)   Italy
(What? direct object)

b) A ME (To whom? Indirect object)   PIACE   (verb)   L'ITALIA
(Who / What? Subject)

You can also say it in another way, but the structure is the same one:
c) MI   (To whom? Indirect object)   PIACE   (verb)   L'ITALIA
(Who / What? Subject)

Note: it is important not to say both together: A ME MI PIACE L'ITALIA. There is a slight difference between b) and c): the first one emphazises the person who likes it:

A ME PIACE L'ITALIA, A TE FORSE NO; while c) is more neutral.

A ME = MI   A ME PIACE L'ITALIA /   MI PIACE
L'ITALIA
A TE = TI   A TE PIACE L'ITALIA /   TI PIACE L'ITALIA
A LUI = GLI   A LUI PIACE L'ITALIA /   GLI PIACE
L'ITALIA
A LEI = LE   A LEI PIACE L'ITALIA /   LE PIACE L'ITALIA
A NOI = CI   A NOI PIACE L'ITALIA /   CI PIACE
L'ITALIA
A VOI = VI   A VOI PIACE L'ITALIA /   VI PIACE
L'ITALIA
A LORO = LORO / GLI   A LORO PIACE L'ITALIA /   GLI PIACE L'ITALIA

Note: if after the verb "to be" there is a verb, instead of a noun, it needs to be in the infinitive form, not preceded by any preposition, e.g.: MI PIACE VISITARE L'ITALIA.

1) Translate the following sentences
   1. She likes playing tennis ....
   2. I like footbal ....
   3. They like going to the cinema ....
   4. We like eating pasta ....
   5. He doesn't like going to school ....

Answers
Chapter 18 Exercise 1

   1. A LEI PIACE GIOCARE A TENNIS
   2. A ME PIACE IL CALCIO
   3. A LORO PIACE ANDARE AL CINEMA
   4. CI PIACE MANGIARE LA PIZZA
   5. NON GLI PIACE ANDARE A SCUOLA

Chapter 19
Past tense: PASSATO PROSSIMO & PASSATO REMOTO

In Italian there are many past tenses; the most common are the PASSATO PROSSIMO and the PASSATO REMOTO. Let's start from the first one.

19.1 PASSATO PROSSIMO

To form the PASSATO PROSSIMO you have to combine the auxiliary (to have or to be) and the past participle of the verb. It is similar to the English "present perfect"; you need it to express something that happened in the past, but not too much time before, and that still have a relationship with the present time:

I've seen that film → IO HO VISTO QUEL FILM

→ How can you choose the auxiliary between ESSERE and AVERE?
The correct auxiliary is almost always the verb AVERE, except for some verbs, often verbs of movement (ANDARE, ARRIVARE, CADERE, TORNARE, DIVENTARE, ...) all reflexive verbs (SVEGLIARSI,...) and impersonal verbs (even if meteorological verbs may use both, with a slight different meaning.

→ How can you form the past participle?

For regular verbs, there are no problem: you just need to add -ATO, -UTO or -ITO depending on the conjugation the verb belongs to (1°, 2° or 3°) to the stem of verb, thus, if the verb in the infinitive ends with -ARE, then you add -ATO; if it ends with -ERE, you add -UTO, and if it ends with -IRE, you add -ITO.

Auxiliary "to have" AVERE	Auxiliary "to be" ESSERE
First conjugation (PARLARE – to speak): IO HO PARL-ATO TU HAI PARL-ATO	First conjugation (ANDARE – to go): IO SONO AND-ATO / A* TU SEI AND-ATO /A LUI / LEI È AND-

LUI / LEI	HA	PARL- ATO
NOI	ABBIAMO	PARL- ATO
VOI	AVETE PARL-	ATO
LORO	HANNO	PARL- ATO

		ATO / A
NOI	SIAMO AND-	ATI / E*
VOI	SIETE AND-	ATI / E
LORO	SONO	AND- ATI / E

Second conjugation (RIPETERE - to repeat)		
IO	HO	RIPET- UTO
TU	HAI	RIPET- UTO
LUI / LEI	HA	RIPET- UTO
NOI	ABBIAMO	RIPET- UTO
VOI	AVETE RIPET-UTO	
LORO	HANNO	RIPET- UTO

Second conjugation (CADERE - to fall)		
IO	SONO	CAD- UTO / A
TU	SEI	CAD- UTO /A
LUI / LEI	È	CAD- UTO / A
NOI	SIAMO CAD-	UTI / E
VOI	SIETE CAD-	UTI / E
LORO	SONO	CAD- UTI / E

Third conjugation (DORMIRE - to sleep)		
IO	HO	DORM- ITO
TU	HAI	DORM- ITO
LUI / LEI	HA	DORM- ITO
NOI	ABBIAMO	DORM- ITO
VOI	AVETE DORM-ITO	
LORO	HANNO	DORM- ITO

Third conjugation (PARTIRE - to depart)		
IO	SONO	PART- ITO / A
TU	SEI	PART- ITO /A
LUI / LEI	È	PART- ITO / A
NOI	SIAMO PART-	ITI / E
VOI	SIETE PART-	ITI / E
LORO	SONO	PART- ITI / E

*Note: as you can see in the table the past participle of all verbs behaves like an adjective <u>if the auxiliary is the verb ESSERE</u>, so you need to conjugate it according to the person (gender and number) you are referring to. E.g.:

He has left → LUI È PARTITO

She has left → LEI È PARTITA

We have left (only girls) → NOI SIAMO PARTITE

We have left (mixed group or only boys) → NOI SIAMO PARTITI

The problem is, as in English, with irregular verbs, that need to be learnt by heart. Here you can see some of the most important Italian irregular verbs.

Infinitive	Past Participle	Auxiliary	Translation
APRIRE	APERTO	AVERE	To open
CHIEDERE	CHIESTO	AVERE	To ask
CHIUDERE	CHIUSO	AVERE	To close
CONOSCERE	CONOSCIUTO	AVERE	To know
CORRERE	CORSO	AVERE	To run
DARE	DATO	AVERE	To give
DIRE	DETTO	AVERE	To say
ESSERE	STATO	ESSERE	To be
FARE	FATTO	AVERE	To do / to make
LEGGERE	LETTO	AVERE	To read
METTERE	MESSO	AVERE	To put
MORIRE	MORTO	ESSERE	To die
NASCERE	NATO	ESSERE	To be born
PERDERE	PERSO	AVERE	To lose
PIACERE	PIACIUTO	ESSERE	To like

PRENDERE	PRESO	AVERE	To take
RIDERE	RISO	AVERE	To laugh
RIMANERE	RIMASTO	ESSERE	To remain
RISPONDERE	RISPOSTO	AVERE	To answer
ROMPERE	ROTTO	AVERE	To break
SCENDERE	SCESO	ESSERE / AVERE*	To get off
SCRIVERE	SCRITTO	AVERE	To write
SPEGNERE	SPENTO	AVERE	To turn off
STARE	STATO	ESSERE	To stay
VEDERE	VISTO	AVERE	To see
VENIRE	VENUTO	ESSERE	To come
VIVERE	VISSUTO	ESSERE / AVERE	To live

* The verb SCENDERE, always needs the auxiliary ESSERE (to be), except when there is a direct object after the verb, e.g.:
I got off → SONO SCESO
I have descended the stairs → IO HO SCESO LE SCALE

1) Complete the text with the following past participle: GUARDATO FATTO ANDATI FINITO DECISO CONOSCIUTO INTITOLATO PREPARATA SEDUTI MANGIATO

UNA VOLTA ………………………… LA CENA, CI SIAMO ………………………… A TAVOLA. ABBIAMO ………………………… UN BEL PIATTO DI SPAGHETTI AL POMODORO E UN PETTO DI POLLO CIASCUNO. DOPO AVER ………………………… SIAMO ………………………… IN SALOTTO E ABBIAMO ………………………… UN BEL FILM COMICO ………………………… IN TUTTO IL MONDO, ………………………… "TUTTI PAZZI PER MARY". DOPO DI CHE, VISTO CHE ORMAI SI ERA ………………………… TARDI, ABBIAMO ………………………… DI ANDARE A LETTO.

2) Study the irregular verbs and then correct the mistakes
    1. IO HO LEGGIUTO LA TUA LETTERA

2. TU HAI PRENDUTO IL RAFFREDDORE
3. NOI ABBIAMO APRITO LA PORTA ALLA SIGNORA
4. LEI HA ANDATA A CASA
5. NOI ABBIAMO RIMASTI A SCUOLA DI POMERIGGIO
6. DANTE   HA SCRIVUTO LA DIVINA COMMEDIA
7. GALILEI HA MORTO NEL SEICENTO
8. NON HAI RISPONDUTO ALLA MIA DOMANDA
9. IO O ACCESO LA LUCE PERCHÉ NON CI VEDEVO
10. IERI HABBIAMO VISTO UN FILM BELLISSIMO

19.2 PASSATO REMOTO

The PASSATO REMOTO is the past tense that indicates an action taken once and completed far in the past; it is more similar to the English "simple past", but each person has a different form. There is no auxiliary:
When I was a child I went to London → DA BAMBINO ANDAI A LONDRA

First conjugation (PARLARE – to speak):

IO	PARL-	AI
TU	PARL-	ASTI
LUI / LEI	PARL-	Ò
NOI	PARL-	AMMO
VOI	PARL-	ASTE
LORO	PARL-	ARONO

Second conjugation (CREDERE - to believe)

IO	CRED-ETTI (-EI)
TU	CRED-ESTI
LUI / LEI	CRED-ETTE (-É)
NOI	CRED-EMMO
VOI	CRED-ESTE
LORO	CRED-ETTERO (ERONO)

Third conjugation (DORMIRE - to sleep)

IO	DORM-II
TU	DORM-ISTI

LUI / LEI	DORM-ì
NOI	DORM-IMMO
VOI	DORM-ISTE
LORO	DORM-IRONO

As for the past participle, also the PASSATO REMOTO has some irregular forms; the most important are:

	AVERE	DARE	DIRE	ESSERE	FARE	METTERE
IO	EBBI	DETTI	DISSI	FUI	FECI	MISI
TU	AVETSI	DESTI	DICESTI	FOSTI	FACESTI	METTESTI
LUI	EBBE	DETTE	DISSE	FU	FECE	MISE
NOI	AVEMMO	DEMMO	DICEMMO	FUMMO	FACEMMO	METTEMMO
VOI	AVESTE	DESTE	DICESTE	FOSTE	FACESTE	METTESTE
LORO	EBBERO	DETTERO	DISSERO	FURONO	FECERO	MISERO

	NASCERE	SCRIVERE	STARE	VEDERE	VENIRE	VIVERE
IO	NACQUI	SCRISSI	STETTI	VIDI	VENNI	VISSI
TU	NASCESTI	SCRIVESTI	STESTI	VEDESTI	VENISTI	VIVESTI
LUI	NACQUE	SCRISSE	STETTE	VIDE	VENNE	VISSE
NOI	NASCEMMO	SCRIVEMMO	STEMMO	VEDEMMO	VENIMMO	VIVEMMO
VOI	NASCESTE	SCRIVESTE	STESTE	VEDESTE	VENISTE	VIVESTE
LORO	NACQUERO	SCRISSERO	STETTERO	VIDERO	VENNERO	VISSERO

3) Complete the story of Little Red Riding Hood (CAPPUCCETTO ROSSO), using the following verbs, that you need to conjugate (tense and person):

PRENDERE – ANDARE – INCONTRARE – INGANNARE – FARE – CORRERE – RAGGIUNGERE – ENTRARE – MANGIARE – ARRIVARE – TROVARE –

RICONOSCERE – AVVICINARE – DIVORARE – PASSARE – SENTIRE – SFONDARE – APRIRE – FARE.

C'ERA UNA VOLTA UNA BAMBINA DI NOME CAPPUCCETTO ROSSO CHE DOVEVA PORTARE DA MANGIARE ALLA NONNA AMMALATA NEL BOSCO. CAPPUCCETTO ROSSO .... IL CESTINO E .... NEL BOSCO. A UN CERTO PUNTO .... UN LUPO CATTIVO CHE LA .... E SI .... DIRE DOVE ABITAVA LA NONNA. IL LUPO .... VELOCISSIMO E .... LA NONNA PRIMA DI CAPPUCETTO ROSSO. IL LUPO .... IN CASA E .... LA NONNA. POCO DOPO .... ANCHE CAPPUCCETTO ROSSO E .... IL LUPO MASCHERATO DA NONNA, NEL LETTO, MA NON LO .... LA BAMBINA SI .... E IL LUPO LA .... PER FORTUNA, ... DI LÌ DEI CACCIATORI CHE .... IL LUPO RUSSARE, COSÌ .... LA PORTA, ... LA PANCIA DEL LUPO, E .... USCIRE LA NONNA E CAPPUCCETTO ROSSO.

4) PASSATO PROSSIMO or PASATO REMOTO? Underline the correct verb

1. IERI HO VISTO / VIDI LA MAMMA DI LUCA

2. DA PICCOLO MARCO SI È ROTTO / RUPPE IL BRACCIO.

3. OGGI A PRANZO MANGIAI / HO MANGIATO UNA BELLA PIZZA

4. LA PRIMA GUERRA MONDIALE È SCOPPIATA / SCOPPIÒ NEL 1914

5. STAMANI SONO ANDATA / ANDAI A LAVORO IN BICICLETTA

6. CRISTOFORO COLOMBO SCOPRÌ / HA SCOPERTO L'AMERICA NEL 1492

7. GLI ANTICHI EGIZI HANNO COSTRUITO / COSTRUIRONO MOLTE PIRAMIDI

8. APPENA ARRIVAI /SONO ARRIVATA A CASA È SQUILLATO IL TELEFONO

9. APPENA ARRIVAI /SONO ARRIVATA A CASA SQUILLÒ IL TELEFONO

10. QUANDO AVEVO 2 ANNI HO DETTO / DISSI LA MIA PRIMA PAROLA

Answers

Chapter 19 Exercise 1

UNA VOLTA PREPARATA LA CENA, CI SIAMO SEDUTI A TAVOLA. ABBIAMO MANGIATO UN BEL PIATTO DI SPAGHETTI AL POMODORO E UN PETTO DI POLLO CIASCUNO. DOPO AVER CENATO SIAMO ANDATI IN SALOTTO E ABBIAMO GUARDATO UN BEL FILM COMICO CONOSCIUTO IN TUTTO IL MONDO, INTITOLATO "TUTTI PAZZI PER MARY". DOPO DI CHE, VISTO CHE ORMAI SI ERA FATTO TARDI, ABBIAMO DECISO DI ANDARE A LETTO.

Chapter 19 Exercise 2

11. IO HO <u>LETTO</u> LA TUA LETTERA

12. TU HAI <u>PRESO</u> IL RAFFREDDORE

13. NOI ABBIAMO <u>APERTO</u> LA PORTA ALLA SIGNORA

14. LEI <u>È</u> ANDATA A CASA

15. NOI <u>SIAMO</u> RIMASTI A SCUOLA DI POMERIGGIO

16. DANTE   HA <u>SCRITTO</u> LA DIVINA COMMEDIA

17. GALILEI <u>È</u> MORTO NEL SEICENTO

18. NON HAI <u>RISPOSTO</u> ALLA MIA DOMANDA

19. IO <u>HO</u> ACCESO LA LUCE PERCHÉ NON CI VEDEVO

20. IERI <u>ABBIAMO</u> VISTO UN FILM BELLISSIMO

Chapter 19 Exercise 3

C'ERA UNA VOLTA UNA BAMBINA DI NOME CAPPUCCETTO ROSSO CHE DOVEVA PORTARE DA MANGIARE ALLA NONNA AMMALATA NEL BOSCO. CAPPUCCETTO ROSSO PRESE IL CESTINO E ANDÒ NEL BOSCO. A UN CERTO PUNTO INCONTRÒ UN LUPO CATTIVO CHE LA INGANNÒ E SI FECE DIRE DOVE ABITAVA LA NONNA. IL LUPO CORSE VELOCISSIMO E RAGGIUNSE LA NONNA PRIMA DI CAPPUCETTO ROSSO. IL LUPO ENTRÒ IN CASA E MANGIÒ LA NONNA. POCO DOPO ARRIVÒ ANCHE CAPPUCCETTO ROSSO E TROVÒ IL LUPO MASCHERATO DA NONNA, NEL LETTO, MA NON LO RICONOBBE. LA BAMBINA SI AVVICINÒ E IL LUPO LA DIVORÒ. PER FORTUNA, PASSARONO DI LÌ DEI CACCIATORI CHE SENTIRONO IL LUPO RUSSARE, COSÌ SFONDARONO LA PORTA, APRIRONO LA PANCIA DEL LUPO, E FECERO USCIRE LA NONNA E CAPPUCCETTO ROSSO.

Chapter 19 Exercise 4

11. IERI <u>HO VISTO</u> / VIDI LA MAMMA DI LUCA
12. DA PICCOLO MARCO SI È ROTTO / <u>RUPPE</u> IL BRACCIO.
13. OGGI A PRANZO MANGIAI / <u>HO MANGIATO</u> UNA BELLA PIZZA
14. LA PRIMA GUERRA MONDIALE È SCOPPIATA / <u>SCOPPIÒ</u> NEL 1914
15. STAMANI <u>SONO ANDATA</u> / ANDAI A LAVORO IN BICICLETTA
16. CRISTOFORO COLOMBO <u>SCOPRÌ</u> / HA SCOPERTO L'AMERICA NEL 1492
17. GLI ANTICHI EGIZI HANNO COSTRUITO / <u>COSTRUIRONO</u> MOLTE PIRAMIDI
18. APPENA ARRIVAI / <u>SONO ARRIVATA</u> A CASA È SQUILLATO IL TELEFONO
19. APPENA <u>ARRIVAI</u> / SONO ARRIVATA A CASA SQUILLÒ IL TELEFONO
20. QUANDO AVEVO 2 ANNI HO DETTO / <u>DISSI</u> LA MIA PRIMA PAROLA

Chapter 20
Future Tense (FUTURO SEMPLICE)

The Italian future tense is different from the English future, because it doesn't need any helping verb as "will"; in Italian a verb ending marks it as being set in the future tense.

To form the FUTURO SEMPLICE you need to remove the -E from the end of the verb (-ARE> -AR-; -ERE> -ER-; -IRE > -IR-), and then you add the suffixes you see in the table below.

First conjugation (PARLARE – to speak)		Second conjugation (CREDERE - to believe)		Third conjugation (DORMIRE - to sleep)	
IO	PARL-ERÒ	IO	CRED-ERÒ	IO	DORM-IRÒ
TU	PARL-ERAI	TU	CRED-ERAI	TU	DORM-IRAI
LUI	PARL-ERÀ	LUI	CRED-ERÀ	LUI	DORM-IRÀ
NOI	PARL-EREMO	NOI	CRED-EREMO	NOI	DORM-IREMO
VOI	PARL-ERETE	VOI	CRED-ERETE	VOI	DORM-IRETE
LORO	PARL-ERANNO	LORO	CRED-ERANNO	LORO	DORM-IRANNO

Obviously there are some exceptions: the irregular verbs. They have a different stem, so you need to attach the suffix to the irregular stem. In the table below you can see the most important ones.

Infinitive	Future stem
ANDARE	ANDR-
AVERE	AVR-
CADERE	CADR-
DOVERE	DOVR-
POTERE	POTR-
SAPERE	SAPR-

VEDERE	VEDR-

Be aware of the spelling of verbs with infinitives ending in -CIARE and -GIARE. These verbs drop the I before adding the future endings to the root, e.g.:

I start – I will start → IO COMIN<u>CI</u>O – IO COMIN<u>CE</u>RÒ
I travel – I will travel → IO VIAG<u>GI</u>O – IO VIAG<u>GE</u>RÒ

And verbs with infinitives ending in -CARE and -GARE add an H to the root for the future to preserve the hard sound of the "c" or "g" of the infinitive:

I look for – I will look for → IO CER<u>CO</u> – IO CER<u>CHE</u>RÒ
I pay – I will pay → IO PA<u>GO</u> – IO PA<u>GHE</u>RÒ

1) Write 10 things the baby will be able to do when he will be retired.

1. QUANDO ANDRÒ IN PENSIONE (SMETTERE DI LAVORARE)
   ....
....

2. (VIAGGIARE MOLTO)
   ....
   ....

3. (GIOCARE CON I MIEI NIPOTI)
....

4. (LEGGERE MOLTI LIBRI)..

5. (ANDARE A PESCARE)..

6. (AVERE MOLTO TEMPO LIBERO)
   ....

7. (VEDRE MOLTI FILM)
   ....

8. (COMPRARE UN BASTONE)
   ....

9. (SAPERE TANTE COSE)

....

10. (VEDERE CHE ESSERE BELLO ANCHE DA VECCHIO)

....
..

Answers
Chapter 20 Exercise 1

1. QUANDO ANDRÒ IN PENSIONE SMETTERÒ DI LAVORARE
2. VIAGGERÒ MOLTO
3. GIOCHERÒ CON I MIEI NIPOTI
4. LEGGERÒ MOLTI LIBRI
5. ANDRÒ A PESCARE
6. AVRÒ MOLTO TEMPO LIBERO
7. VEDRÒ MOLTI FILM
8. COMPRERÒ UN BASTONE
9. SAPRÒ TANTE COSE
10. VEDRÒ CHE SARÒ BELLO ANCHE DA VECCHIO

PART 3

USEFUL VOCABULARY

In this chapter you will learn the names of the main parts of the body. Many of them have an irregular plural form. In some cases, moreover, the word is masculine in the singular form and feminine in the plural form, e.g.: IL BRACCIO (masculine), LE BRACCIA (feminine). For this reason you can see, for each word, both the singular and the plural form, together with the article.

21.1 The body _ IL CORPO

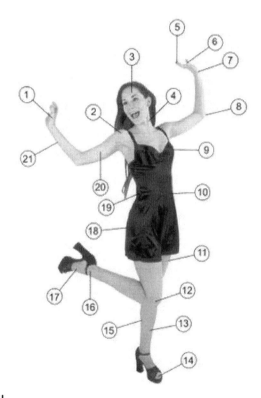

1. LA MANO – LE MANI
2. LA SPALLA – LE SPALLE
3. LA TESTA – LE TESTE
4. IL COLLO – I COLLI
5. IL DITO – LE DITA
6. IL PALMO – I PALMI
7. IL POLSO – I POLSI
8. IL GOMITO – I GOMITI

9. IL SENO – I SENI (for women) / IL PETTO – I PETTI (for both women and men)
10. LA PANCIA – LE PANCE
11. LA GAMBA – LE GAMBE (the upper part is LA COSCIA – LE COSCE)
12. IL GINOCCHIO – LE GINOCCHIA
13. LO STINCO – GLI STINCHI
14. IL DITO (DEL PIEDE) – LE DITA (DEL PIEDE)
15. IL POLPACCIO – I POLPACCI
16. LA CAVIGLIA – LE CAVIGLIE
17. IL PIEDE – I PIEDI
18. IL SEDERE – I SEDERI
19. IL FIANCO – I FIANCHI
20. IL BRACCIO – LE BRACCIA
21. L'AVAMBRACCIO – GLI AVAMBRACCI

21.2 The face (IL VISO / LA FACCIA)

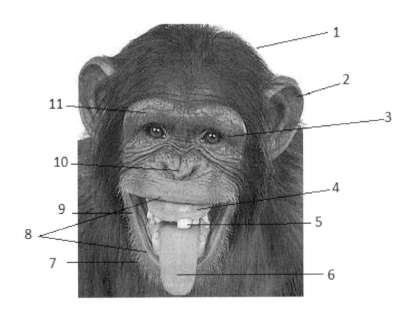

1. IL CAPELLO – I CAPELLI
2. L'ORECCHIO – LE ORECCHIE
3. L'OCCHIO – GLI OCCHI

4. LA GENGIVA – LE GENGIVE
5. IL DENTE – I DENTI
6. LA LINGUA – LE LINGUE
7. LA BARBA – LE BARBE
8. IL LABBRO – LE LABBRA
9. LA BOCCA – LE BOCCHE
10. IL NASO – I NASI
11. IL SOPRACCIGLIO – LE SOPRACCIGLIA

1) Draw the monster described below:

IL MOSTRO HA DUE TESTE CHE POGGIANO SU DUE COLLI LUNGHISSIMI. HA I CAPELLI LUNGHI LISCI, DI COLORE VIOLA. HA UN OCCHIO IN OGNI FACCIA. GLI OCCHI SONO ROSSI E MOLTO PICCOLI. IL NASO È LUNGO E SOTTILE. LA BOCCA ENORME, CON MOLTI DENTI CHE ESCONO DI FUORI. IL MOSTRO HA SEI BRACCIA MOLTO CORTE, E SEI GAMBE MOLTO LUNGHE E MAGRE. LE MANI E I PIEDI HANNO QUATTRO DITA CIASCUNO.

2) Describe the man / woman of your dream (L'UOMO / LA DONNA DEI MIEI SOGNI), using as many terms as you can, from those you have just read in the pictures above. Remember to use the colors and the adjectives you have already studied.

21.3 The diseases (LE MALATTIE)

INFLUENZA	Flu
FEBBRE	Temperature
RAFFREDDORE	Cold
TOSSE	Cough
MAL DI GOLA	Sore throat
MAL DI TESTA	Headache
MAL DI PANCIA	Bellyache
MAL DI STOMACO	Stomach-ache
MAL DI DENTI	Toothache
VOMITO / NAUSEA	Vomit / Nausea
DIARREA	Diarrhoea
TORCICOLLO	Stiff neck
INSONNIA	Insomnia
FRATTURA	Fracture
ROTTURA	Break

3) Put one word from the list in each sentence. Use each word once only.

MAL DI TESTA – FEBBRE – MAL DI GOLA – MAL DI DENTI – FRATTURA –
TOSSE – RAFFREDDORE – NASO – TORCICOLLO – INSONNIA

1. ODIO ANDARE DAL DENTISTA, MA CON QUESTO ....
   NON POSSO PROPRIO FARNE A MENO.
2. QUANDO NON RIESCO A DORMIRE MOLTO, MI SVEGLIO SEMPRE CON
   IL ....
3. TI HO DETTO DI NON USCIRE DI CASA SENZA LA GIACCA. COSÌ TI
   VERRÀ LA ....
4. MARTA   È CADUTA DAL CAVALLO E HA RIPORTATO UNA
   .... AL POLSO.

5. STAMATTINA MI SONO SVEGLIATO CON UN FORTE
.................................; PROBABILMENTE HO DORMITO IN UNA
BRUTTA POSIZIONE.

6. DEVI SMETTERE DI FUMARE, SENNÒ LA .... NON TI
ANDRÀ MAI PIÙ VIA.

7. SE HAI IL .... MOLTO FORTE POSSO CONSIGLIARTI
DELLE CARAMELLE MOLTO EFFICACI.

8. L'INGESTIONE PUÒ CAUSARE .... , ... E
....

9. LUIGI HA LA VOCE NASALE: SEMBRA CHE ABBIA SEMPRE IL
....

10. È INUTILE CHE PRENDO LA CAMOMILLA, IN QUESTO PERIODO NON
RIESCO MAI A DORMIRE. MI SA CHE COMINCIO A SOFFRIRE DI
....

Answers

Chapter 21 Exercise 3

1. MAL DI DENTI
2. MAL DI TESTA
3. FEBBRE
4. FRATTURA
5. TORCICOLLO
6. TOSSE
7. MAL DI GOLA
8. NAUSEA – VOMITO – DIARREA
9. RAFFREDDORE
10. INSONNIA

Chapter 22: My Clothes

IL CALZINO / I CALZINI

LA MAGLIA / LE MAGLIE

IL JEANS / I JEANS

LA SCARPA / LE SCARPE

LA CAMICIA / LE CAMICIE

LA CINTURA / LE CINTURE (LA/E CINTOLA / E)

IL COMPLETO (LA GIACCA E IL PANTALONE)

L CAPPELLO / I CAPPELLI
LA BORSA / LE BORSE
GLI OCCHIALI (DA SOLE)
LE SCARPE
IL VESTITO / I VESTITI

LE CALZE

1) What are these people wearing? Answer the question, talking about their clothes, colors and length (long = LUNGO; short = CORTO)

LA RAGAZZA INDOSSA ....

IL RAGAZZO INDOSSA ....

IL SIGNORE INDOSSA ....

Answers

Chapter 22 Exercise 1

LA RAGAZZA INDOSSA UN VESTITO LUNGO, VERDE SCURO, CON UNA CINTOLA BIANCA. HA LE CALZE NERE E LE SCARPE NERE. AL COLLO PORTA UNA BELLA COLLANA.

IL RAGAZZO INDOSSA UN PAIO DI PANTALONI CORTI BLU, UNA MAGLIA A MANICHE CORTE CELESTE, I CALZINI LUNGHI E CELESTI   E LE SCARPE DA GINNASTICA ROSSE, BIANCHE E NERE.

IL SIGNORE INDOSSA UNA CAMICIA BIANCA, CON SOPRA UNA GIACCA BLU. NON PORTA LA CRAVATTA. INDOSSA UN PAIO DI PANTALONI LUNGHI BLU SCURO, UNA CINTURA MARRONE E UN PAIO DI SCARPE MARRONI.

Chapter 23
My House

LA CASA	House
IL TETTO	Roof
LA PORTA	Door
IL COMIGNOLO	Chimney
LA STANZA	Room
LA FINESTRA	Window
LA CUCINA	Kitchen
LA SALA / IL SALOTTO	Living room
IL BAGNO	Bathroom
LA CAMERA (DA LETTO)	Bedroom
LO STUDIO	Studio
IL GARAGE	Garage
LA CABINA ARMADIO	Walk-in closet
LA SOFFITTA	Attic
LA CATINA	Cellar
IL RIPOSTIGLIO	Utility room
IL TAVOLO	Table

LA SEDIA	Chair
LA CULLA	Cradle
PIANO TERRA / TERRENO	Ground floor
PRIMO PIANO	First floor
ULTIMO PIANO	Top floor
GLI ELETTRODOMESTICI	Domestic appliance

1) Correct the mistakes in the description of the house, looking at the picture above.

LA CASA È DISPOSTA SU TRE PIANI: PIANO TERRA, PRIMO PIANO E TERZO PIANO. AL PIANO TERRA CI SONO DUE GARAGE CON UNA MACCHINA MARRONE.

AL PIANO TERRA SI TROVANO ANCHE LE DUE CAMERE E IL BAGNO. LA SALA È AL PRIMO PIANO, ACCANTO ALLA CABINA ARMADIO. LA CUCINA NON HA FINESTRE, MA HA MOLTI ELETTRODOMESTICI. ALL'ULTIMO PIANO SI TROVA UNO STUDIO CON UN DIVANO, UNA TELEVISIONE E UNA GROSSA LAMPADA. ACCANTO ALLO STUDIO C'È UNA SOFFITTA. NON C'È NESSUNA CAMERA PER BAMBINI. SUL TETTO C' È UN COMIGNOLO.

2) And now describe your house.

Answers

Chapter 23 Exercise 1

LA CASA È DISPOSTA SU TRE PIANI: PIANO TERRA, PRIMO PIANO E SECONDO PIANO. AL PIANO TERRA C'È UN GARAGE CON UNA MACCHINA BLU.
AL PIANO TERRA SI TROVANO ANCHE LA SALA E LA CUCINA. LE DUE CAMERE SONO AL PRIMO PIANO, ACCANTO ALLA CABINA ARMADIO E AL BAGNO. LA CUCINA HA UNA FINESTRA, MA HA MOLTI ELETTRODOMESTICI. ALL'ULTIMO PIANO SI TROVA UNO STUDIO CON UN DIVANO, UNA TELEVISIONE E UNA GROSSA LAMPADA. ACCANTO ALLO STUDIO C'È UNA SOFFITTA. C'È UNA CAMERA PER BAMBINI. SUL TETTO C' È UN COMIGNOLO.

Chapter 24: At The Restaurant

If you are in a restaurant and you want to order something to eat, you can use the conditional tense of the verb VOLERE (to want), i.e.: VORREI (I would like).

IO	VORREI
TU	VORRESTI
LUI / LEI	VORREBBE
NOI	VORREMMO
VOI	VORRESTE
LORO	VORREBBERO

1) Read the dialog below and underline the words or expressions that are used to order something.

CLIENTE: BUONGIORNO, VORREI UN TAVOLO PER DUE, PER FAVORE.

CAMERIERE: BUONGIORNO, ECCO QUA SIGNORI.

CLIENTE: POSSO VEDERE IL MENÙ PER FAVORE? AVETE UNA SPECIALITÀ DELLA CASA?

CAMERIERE: SI SIGNORE, LA NOSTRA SPECIALITÀ È LA CARNE ALLA FIORENTINA.

CLIENTE: È POSSIBILE AVERE UN CIBO VEGETARIANO?

CAMERIERE: POSSO PORTARLE UNA BUONA INSALATA E DEI CROSTINI MISTI.

CLIENTE: PERFETTO. MIA MOGLIE VORREBBE ASSAGGIARE LA FIORENTINA.

CAMERIERE: VA BENISSIMO. DA BERE COSA VI PORTO?

CLIENTE: VORREMMO UNA BOTTIGLIA DI CHIANTI CLASSICO.

CAMERIERE: SOLO UN MOMENTO E ARRIVA TUTTO. BUON APPETITO!

Here you can learn some useful expressions to use in bars and restaurants

SCUSI, CAMERIERE?(M)/CAMERIERA?	Excuse me, waiter?
UN TAVOLO PER UNO/DUE, PER FAVORE.	A table for one person/two people, please.
POSSO VEDERE IL MENU, PER FAVORE?	Can I look at the menu, please?
C'È UNA SPECIALITÀ LOCALE?	Is there a local specialty?
SONO VEGETARIANO/A	I'm a vegetarian.
PRANZO A PREZZO FISSO	fixed-price meal
À LA CARTE	à la carte
POSSO AVERE UN BICCHIERE / UNA BOTTIGLIA DI...?	May I have a glass / a bottle of ...?
ERA BUONISSIMO / DELIZIOSO!	It was delicious!
IL CONTO, PER FAVORE.	The bill, please.
C'È IL SERVIZIO AL TAVOLO?	Is there table service?

2) And now try to guess which kind of meal you are going to have:
COLAZIONE, PRANZO, MERENDA, CENA.

1. You are tired, but a delicious .... is waiting for you at home!
2. It's four p.m. and you are a bit hungry. You don't manage to wait till this evening, so you decide to have ....
3. It's one o'clock. Now you can stop working and have your ....
4. You have just woken up and you eat for the first time in the day, you are having..................

What would you like to have for breakfast?

VORREI DEL CAFFÈ

VORREI UN PO' DI LATTE

VORREI UNA TAZZA DI TÈ

VORREI DEI BISCOTTI

And for lunch and dinner?

LA PASTA

LA CARNE

IL PANE

IL FORMAGGIO

IL POLLO

L'UOVO _ LE UOVA

IL PESCE

L'ACQUA

LE PATATINE FRITTE

But what I prefer is the.... dessert!

IL DOLCE

LA TORTA

IL GELATO

3) Write what you generally have for breakfast, for lunch and for dinner.

A COLAZIONE DI SOLITO MANGIO ....

A / PER PRANZO ....

A / PER CENA ....

Answers

Chapter 24 Exercise 1

CLIENTE: BUONGIORNO, <u>VORREI</u> UN TAVOLO PER DUE, PER FAVORE.

CAMERIERE: BUONGIORNO, ECCO QUA SIGNORI.

CLIENTE: <u>POSSO</u> VEDERE IL MENÙ PER FAVORE? <u>AVETE</u> UNA SPECIALITÀ DELLA CASA?

CAMERIERE: SI SIGNORE, LA NOSTRA SPECIALITÀ È LA CARNE ALLA FIORENTINA.

CLIENTE: <u>È POSSIBILE AVERE</u> UN CIBO VEGETARIANO?

CAMERIERE: POSSO PORTARLE UNA BUONA INSALATA E DEI CROSTINI MISTI.

CLIENTE: PERFETTO. MIA MOGLIE <u>VORREBBE</u> ASSAGGIARE LA FIORENTINA.

CAMERIERE: VA BENISSIMO. DA BERE COSA VI PORTO?

CLIENTE: <u>VORREMMO</u> UNA BOTTIGLIA DI CHIANTI CLASSICO.

CAMERIERE: SOLO UN MOMENTO E ARRIVA TUTTO. BUON APPETITO!

Chapter 24 exercise 2

1) CENA
2) MERENDA
3) PRANZO

4) COLAZIONE

Chapter 25
Travel And Holidays

If you are travelling around Italy by public transportation, the following table will be very useful for you!

QUANTO COSTA UN BIGLIETTO PER...?	How much is a ticket to .....?
UN BIGLIETTO PER..., PER FAVORE.	One ticket to ....., please.
DOVE VA QUESTO TRENO / QUEST'AUTOBUS?	Where does this train/bus go?
QUESTO TRENO/QUEST'AUTOBUS SI FERMA A ..... ?	Does this train/bus stop in ....?
DOV'È IL TRENO/L'AUTOBUS PER	Where is the train/bus to ....?
QUANDO PARTE IL TRENO/L'AUTOBUS PER	When does the train/bus for .... leave?
QUANDO ARRIVA A ..... QUESTO TRENO/QUEST'AUTOBUS?	When will this train/bus arrive in....?

And if you get lost, you may need the following sentences!

COME SI ARRIVA A ...... ?	How do I get to .....?
...ALLA STAZIONE FERROVIARIA?	...to the railway station?
...ALLA STAZIONE DELL'AUTOBUS?	...to the bus station?
...ALL'AEROPORTO?	...to the airport?
...IN CENTRO?	...downtown?
POTETE MOSTRARMELO SULLA CARTA?	Can you show (it to) me on the map?
GIRI A SINISTRA.	Turn left.
GIRI A DESTRA.	Turn right.

VADA A DIRITTO	Go straight ahead
TAXI! MI PORTA A ...., PER FAVORE.	Taxi! Take me to ... , please.
QUANTO COSTA ANDARE A ....?	How much does it cost to get to ....?
VADO DI FRETTA! / HO FRETTA!	I'm in a hurry!
PER FAVORE, MI PORTI A....	Please take me to.....
SI FERMI QUI, PER FAVORE.	Stop here, please.

But when you finally find your hotel, you need to ask for the following things:

AVETE CAMERE LIBERE?	Do you have any rooms available?
QUANTO COSTA UNA STANZA SINGOLA/DOPPIA?	How much is a room for one person/two people?
LA STANZA HA ...	Does the room come with...
LENZUOLA	bed sheets
UN BAGNO	A bathroom
UN TELEFONO	A telephone
POSSO PRIMA VEDERE LA STANZA?	May I see the room first?
VA BENE, LA PRENDO.	OK, I'll take it.
AVETE UNA CASSAFORTE	Do you have a safe?
È INCLUSA LA COLAZIONE / LA CENA?	Is breakfast/supper included?
A CHE ORA È LA COLAZIONE / LA CENA?	What time is breakfast/supper?
PULITE LA MIA CAMERA, PER FAVORE.	Please clean my room.
ACCETTATE CARTE DI CREDITO?	Do you accept credit cards?
DOVE POSSO CAMBIARE DEL DENARO?	Where can I get money changed?
QUANT'È IL CAMBIO?	What is the exchange rate?

DOVE POSSO TROVARE UN BANCOMAT?	Where is an ATM machine?

1) How can the aunt get to his fiancé? Help him with simple instructions.

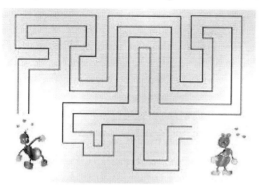

LE VACANZE

LA MONTAGNA

IL MARE

1) Comprehension: read the text and answer the questions

LA MONTAGNA O IL MARE?

SCEGLIERE IL MARE O LA MONTAGNA COME LUOGO DOVE PASSARE LE VACANZE ESTIVE NON È SEMPLICISSIMO, E SOPRATTUTTO È UNA SCELTA INTERIORE, CHE SVELA, IN PARTE, IMPORTANTI TRATTI PSICOLOGICI DELLA NOSTRA PERSONA, DEI NOSTRI PENSIERI, DEL NOSTRO MODO DI VIVERE, IN BREVE, DEL NOSTRO CARATTERE.

IL MARE E LA MONTAGNA SONO PER ECCELLENZA DUE OPPOSTI E QUESTA CONTRAPPOSIZIONE SI RISPECCHIA FEDELMENTE NELLE MENTI DI COLORO CHE SCELGONO L'UNA O L'ALTRA COSA. LA MONTAGNA CI RICORDA IL FREDDO, IL SILENZIO, LA QUIETE, MA SOPRATTUTTO LA SOLITUDINE. LA MONTAGNA È SOLO SILENZIO SOLITUDINE E GHIACCIO. IL MARE INVECE CI FA PENSARE AL CALORE, AL SOLE E ALLA GENTE, AL DIVERTIMENTO E ALLA GIOIA DI VIVERE.

MA NON È TUTTO: LA SOLITUDINE NON SEMPRE È UNA COSA NEGATIVA: IL SELENZIO, LA PACE, LA TRAQUILLITÀ SPESSO CI AIUTANO A RILASSARCI, MENTRE LA GENTE, LA CONFUSIONE E IL CALDO A VOLTE CI RENDONO NERVOSI.

QUINDI LASCIO A VOI LA SCELTA: MARE O MONTAGNA?

A) QUALE DELLE DUE METE PREFERISCE L'AUTORE? PERCHÉ?
....
....
B) E TU, QUALE META PREFERISCI? PERCHÉ?
....
....

Answers

Chapter 25 Exercise 1

VAI A DIRITTO, GIRA A DESTRA, GIRA A SINISTRA, GIRA A SINISTRA, GIRA A DESTRA,   GIRA A DESTRA, GIRA A DESTRA, GIRA A DESTRA, VAI A DIRITTO, ARRIVA FINO IN FONDO ALLA STRADA E GIRA A SINISTRA, POI DI NUOVO A SINISTRA E ANCORA A SINISTRA. SVOLTA A DESTRA, SVOLTA DI NUOVO A

DESTRA, SVOLTA SINISTRA NELLE TRE STRADE SUCCESSIVE, E POI A DESTRA CINQUE VOLTE. GIRA DUE VOLTE A SINISTRA E VAI FINO IN FONDO ALLA VIA. SVOLTA A DESTRA E POI SUBITO A SINISTRA. GIRA A SINISTRA, POI A DESTRA, A SINISTRA DUE VOLTE E ANCORA A DESTRA   DUE VOLTE. SVOLTA DUE VOLTE A SINISTRA E, INFINE, SVOLTANDO PER L'ULTIMA VOLTA A DESTRA, TROVI LA TUA FIDANZATA.

Chapter 25 Exercise 2

A) L'AUTORE NON HA UNA PREFERENZA PERCHÉ CIASCUNA DELLE DUE METE HA DEI PREGI E DEI DIFETTI.

B) IO PREFERISCO LA VACANZA IN MONTAGNA / AL MARE
PERCHÉ........................

Conclusion
Now, Embark on Your Own Adventure!

Now you are ready to go out there and start communicating in the basic Italian that you have learned from this book. Keep in mind that you have not learned how to say *everything* in Italian, but you are equipped to make a great start and work your way around using what you now know. Don't forget the basic language skills that you have learned in this book. If you don't know how to say something, ask, use context clues, describe it using the language that you know, and you will eventually find the answer.

Don't worry about looking silly and just do your best to learn from the mistakes you make! Keep a journal to write about your experiences and the new things that you are learning every day. Though it's not always easy and sometimes rather frustrating, traveling abroad is one of the most rewarding experiences you will have. I hope this book has prepared you well and wish you many exciting and fulfilling adventures in your travels!

To your success,

Dagny Taggart

>> Get The Full Italian Online Course With Audio Lessons <<

If you truly want to learn Italian 300% FASTER, then hear this out.

I've partnered with the most revolutionary language teachers to bring you the very best Italian online course I've ever seen. It's a mind-blowing program specifically created for language hackers such as ourselves. It will allow you learn Italian 3x faster, straight from the comfort of your own home, office, or wherever you may be. It's like having an unfair advantage!

The Online Course consists of:

+ 183 Built-In Lessons
+ 95 Interactive Audio Lessons
+ 24/7 Support to Keep You Going

The program is extremely engaging, fun, and easy-going. You won't even notice you are learning a complex foreign language from scratch. And before you realize it, by the time you go through all the lessons you will officially become a truly solid Italian speaker.

Old classrooms are a thing of the past. It's time for a language revolution.

If you'd like to go the extra mile, follow the link below and let the revolution begin!

>> http://www.bitly.com/Italian-Course <<

CHECK OUT THE COURSE »

PS: Can I Ask You a Quick Favor?

If you liked the book, please leave a nice review on Amazon! I'd absolutely love to hear your feedback. Every time I read your reviews... you make me smile. Please go to Amazon right now (following the link below), and write down a quick line sharing with me your experience. I personally read ALL the reviews there, and I'm thrilled to hear your feedback and honest motivation. It's what keeps me going, and helps me improve everyday =)

Go to Amazon following the link below and write a quick review!

>> http://www.amazon.com/Italian-Ultimate-Course-Learning-Language-ebook/dp/B00KLDHL4O/ <<

***

ONCE YOU'RE BACK,
FLIP THE PAGE!
BONUS CHAPTER AHEAD
=)

Preview Of "Italian For Tourists - The Most Essential Italian Guide to Travel Abroad, Meet People & Find Your Way Around - All While Speaking Perfect Italian!"

Introduction
Prepare Yourself, We're About to Depart!

Tourism in Italy is a very ancient practice: in the late 17th century aristocrats used to go to Italy during the Grand Tour, to refine their knowledge and increase their culture, and still today Italy is one of the best-known countries all over the world, where tens of thousands of tourists travel to, every year, especially for its history, culture, art, cuisine, fashion and nature.

Italy is the country with the highest number of World Heritage Sites in the world (50 out of 1001).

On the other hand, the Italians are a population of travel lovers: you can find them all over the world, and also for this reason it is not so difficult to know some Italian words, such as GRAZIE and BUONGIORNO. Despite that, not many Italian people speak English very well, even though English is a compulsory subject they study at school since the elementary school (except older people, who sometimes used to study French). Also for this reason they will understand your difficulty with a foreign language, and they will try to help you, struggling to find out what you are trying to say, and answering to you with some English words, probably with an absurd grammar, and, above all, gesticulating.

Nonetheless, learning some words, and a bit of the culture of the place you are going to visit is a sign of respect and friendship towards the country and the people you are going to meet, and Italian people always appreciate the effort of a stranger that tries to speak their language. For an Italian person it is not very common to hear a foreigner that speaks Italian; they are aware of the fact that despite the great past they have had, nowadays the Italian language is only spoken in Italy and in few other small countries, so they will be positively surprised by your skills.

Reading this book you will have the opportunity to learn the most important words and sentences you can use when you are travelling around Italy, for both holidays and business. In fact, this phrase book covers expressions related to travel, business, everyday life, food and drinks, social events, meeting new people and introducing yourself. You will have the opportunity to study first, and, then, to put yourself to the test, making the exercises you find at the end of each chapter, and looking, then, at the solutions.

Chapter 1
Getting Around Italian on a Few Bites

A Bite of Italian Geography, History & Dialects

The Italian Peninsula is located in the southern part of Europe and is divided into 20 regions, some of which are very famous all over the world, such as Tuscany (Toscana), Sicily (Sicilia) and Sardinia (Sardegna).

Within any region there are many different dialects: sometimes one for each city or even small village. There is only one region in Italy that has no dialect: Tuscany. Actually in the past there was a dialect in Tuscany too, but for cultural, economic and historical reasons, the Tuscan dialect became the Italian language, thus, we could say that the Italian language is the Tuscan dialect – even if today there are a few exceptions especially in the pronunciation of some letters and words. Why did the Tuscan dialect win against all the other dialects? Let's go back to the Latin language! In the Roman times, there were two kinds of Latin languages: the written one and the spoken one. With the fall of the Western Roman Empire and the formation of the Roman-Barbarian kingdoms, the written language became the administrative language, while the spoken Latin merges deeply with the local dialects, creating new languages, the so-called "volgari" languages. Dante started writing in the Tuscan language – in the "Volgare Toscano" – instead of Latin, that was the only language used to write, but that was also completely unknown to non-educated people. Thanks to Dante, even "common" people, could start to learn how to write and read, because someone was finally writing the language they could understand.

In the 14th century, the amazing literary production of the great Tuscan poets such as Dante Alighieri, Giovanni Boccaccio and Francesco Petrarca had an extraordinary influence on literature all over Italy, so that the Tuscan dialect spread to most of the Peninsula. In fact, some writers from other regions started using it too, for example Sannazzaro from Naples, and Boiardo from Emilia Romagna.

The Italian language was born, but already from the end of the 14th century, the "Volgare Toscano" changed a little bit, detaching from the official language. For many centuries, till not so long ago – for example when my grandmother was a child – the Italian people used to speak their dialect, and the Italian language was like a foreign language they had to learn at school (if they used to go to school).

Until the second half of the 19th century only few people were able to speak Italian.

In 1861 there was the proclamation of the kingdom of Italy: for the first time the Italian Peninsula was not a combination of different countries, with different languages, customs and traditions, but it was ONE united nation, with ONE national language... in theory! In fact it was like this only on paper, because according to the linguist Tullio De Mauro only 2.5% of the Italian population used to speak Italian (10% according to linguist and philologist Arrigo Castellani).

Nowadays everybody speaks Italian, and dialects are only used to speak in very informal situations, within the family, with friends, mostly for jokes and common sayings, and in some regions only the older people know and speak the dialect.

There are some places where the language is strongly influenced by the bordering countries, for example in Trentino Alto Adige (North-East) people speaks German very well (sometimes better than Italian!), and they speak Italian with a German accent while in Valle d'Aosta (North-West) the accent is more similar to the French language, and the French language is the official language together with Italian.

Countries where Italian is spoken

Italian is spoken as a native and official language in 4 countries: Italy (59 million people), Switzerland, San Marino and Vatican City and it is the second official language in Malta, Slovenia and Croatia (for a total of 14 million people).

And now, let's start! And... don't worry, you are not going to learn all the Italian dialects but just the real Italian language!!!

A Bite of Italian Pronunciation

In the first chapters you are going to see the pronunciation of each word and sentence, so that you will be able not only to learn the sentences, but also to say them in the correct way. The Italian language has a very simple pronunciation: they read the words as they write them, only with a few exceptions. So you just need to have a look of the following table, in which you can find the symbols that are going to be used further to write the Italian sounds of each letter.

Note that some vowels have two different pronunciations (closed, for example "▨", and open for example "o"), but the meaning of the word hardly ever changes, in fact even Italian people, depending on the region they are from, say the words in both ways, without any misunderstanding, or change of meaning.
On the other hand, it is important to learn the pronunciation of a few consonants (C, G and S) that have different sounds depending on the preceding or following letters, because in this case people will not understand what you are saying.

a	[a]	cat
b	[b]	bad
c		
c + a / o / u; ch + e; ch + i	[ka / ko / ku]; [ke / kɛ]; [ki]	car; chemistry; kick
c + e; c + i	[tʃe]; [tʃi]	cherry; chip
ci + a; ci + o; ci + u	[tʃa]; [tʃo]; [tʃu]	chance; choice; chew
d	[d]	dance
e	[æ]	bag

	[e]	bed
f	[f]	flower
G		
g + a / o / u; gh + e; gh + i	[ga / go / gu]; [ge / gɛ]; [gi]	gun; game; give
g + e; g + i	[dʒe]; [dʒi]	gentle; ginger
gi + a; gi + o; gi + u	[dʒa]; [dʒo]; [dʒu]	jar; job; july
g + li	[ʎ]	(a bit like "billion", or the Spanish "ll")
gli	[gli]	glimmer
gn	[ɲ]	(a bit like "menu", but stronger, or the Spanish "ñ")
h		not pronounced
i	[i]	thing
l	[l]	love
m	[m]	mother
n	[n]	nose
o	[o] [ɔ]	call lot
p	[p]	pet
q(u)	[ku]	quick
r	[r]	red, but stronger (as the Spanish "r")
S		
s	s	silence
s	z	zebra
sc + e; sc + i	[ʃe]; [ʃi]	share; shift

sci + a / o / u	[ʃa / o / u]	shut; show; shoot
sc + consonant	[sk]	school
t	[t]	tea
u	[u]	food
v	[v]	violet
z	[ts] [dz]	hits dziggetai

Double letters and accent

Maybe you have noticed that the Italian language is very melodious, and it depends also on the fact that there are many "double letters" together, that create a special rhythm in the word, and in the sentence. If you don't stress that letter, the word will often have a different meaning. This stress is represented by the colon ":".

Here you can see how the meaning changes if you forget to double the letter:

PALLA ['pal:a] = Ball	but	PALA ['pala] = Shovel
CASSA ['cas:a] = Cash register / case	but	CASA ['casa] = Home
ROSSA ['ros:a] = Red (female)	but	ROSA ['rosa] = Rose / Pink
CARRO ['car:o] = Cart	but	CARO ['caro] = Dear
PAPPA ['pap:a] = Baby food (familiar)	but	PAPA ['papa] = Pope

Another important thing you may have noticed is this symbol '

It is used to indicate the stressed syllable, and it stresses the first following vowel, so in 'PALLA, for example, the accent is on the first "a".

Generally the stressed syllable is the second to last. If it is the last one, you will find an accent on the vowel, e.g., "papà" (dad), "città" (city), but if it is the third to last , e.g., "perdere" (to lose) you have to look it up in a dictionary, because there won't be any mark on it.

A Bite of Italian Structure

There are a few rules you have to keep in mind, about the structure of the Italian language:

A) The basic form is:

<u>SUBJECT</u> (not always necessary*) + <u>VERB</u> (the action that is happening) + <u>OBJECT</u>

* Italian is a "null-subject language", i.e. a language whose grammar permits an independent clause to lack an explicit subject. Null-subject languages express person, number, and/or gender agreement with the referent on the verb, rendering a subject noun phrase redundant. Especially the subject "IO" ("I") is often dropped because the suffix of the verb tells you who is the subject, e.g. "IO PARL<u>O</u> – TU PARL<u>I</u>" (I <u>speak</u> – you <u>speak</u>) is already conjugated to show if it's "I" or "you", and so on. Thus, you can just say "PARLO ITALIANO" instead of "IO PARLO ITALIANO", and people clearly understand that the subject is "IO". (Anyway it is not a mistake if you say it). You can also say it if you want to emphasize the subject, e.g., IO PARLO ITALIANO, (I SPEAK ITALIAN) stresses the fact that it is me who can speak Italian, not you or the friend of mine.

B) ADJECTIVES GENERALLY FOLLOW THE WORD THEY ARE DESCRIBING:

Red pen = PENNA ROSSA

C) You can use the POSSESSIVE ADJECTIVE together with the ARTICLE:
ARTICLE + POSSESSIVE ADJECTIVE + SUBJECT + ADJECTIVE
My red pen = LA MIA PENNA ROSSA

A Bite of Italian Culture

Cultural Identity

What is strange to say is that in the course of time Italy hasn't found a cultural unit. It is still divided into three main areas: the North, the Centre and the South, that are very different from each other. Obviously it is just a matter of stereotypes, but if we would summarize the North with a few words we could think of: business, fog, prosperity, parties, fashion, snob; while the South is more related to the following terms: family, traditions, poverty, sun, food and unfortunately organized crime. There is even a derogatory term used by Northern Italians to describe Southern Italians: TERRONE, from the word TERRA "earth", meaning that the Southern Italians are illiterate and ignorant and can only work the land.

In this picture you can roughly see the border of the three areas in which "the Boot" is divided.

Maybe one of the few moments in which a Southern and a Northern Italian feel they are living in the same nation is when the world football championship is on!

Popular traditions and practices

Except for the Patron Saint's Day, which is different in any city, and is celebrated with different practices – among which a procession along the streets of the city centre or close to the church dedicated to the Saint, with the statue or a relic of the Saint him- / herself – almost all festivities are celebrated in the same way all over Italy. Let's start from January!

→ Capodanno [kapo'dan:o]

The years begin with a festivity in Italy! "Il primo dell'anno", literally "the first of the year" people get up late and just relax or visit their family and friends. In fact, many people celebrate New Year's Eve till late at night, going to parties, or to friend's homes, or having a ski holiday, and it is the occasion to drink lots of sparkling wine and champagne and to wish each other all the best for the coming year. In each city there are public fireworks organized by the Municipality, and also many individual people like shooting them with friends.

Public life is generally quiet in Italy on January 1st. Post offices, banks, stores and other businesses are closed. Outside of tourist areas, restaurants and cafés may be closed.

→ Epifania [epifa'nia]

This is a Christian holy day on January 6th that celebrates the day when the Three Kings came to see the baby Jesus. Throughout Italy its symbol is the "Befana": an ugly, old woman that flies on a broom, bringing sweets to good children and coal to bad children on Epiphany Eve (the night of January 5th). It is another occasion for families to spend a day together and have a festive lunch with relatives.

There is a nice poem about Befana that children often study at school. You can learn it by heart and tell it to Italian children. They will hope that you are bringing them a sweet!
Here you can also find the English translation:

La Befana vien di notte Con le scarpe tutte rotte Col vestito alla romana Viva, Viva La Befana!	[la be'fana vi'en di not:e] [kon le 'skarpe tut:e rot:e] [kol ve'stito alla ro'mana] ['viva 'viva la be'fana]	The Befana comes by night With her shoes all tattered and torn She comes dressed in the Roman way Long life to the Befana!

→ La festa della donna [la 'festa del:a 'don:a]

It is the Women's day: 8 Marzo ['ot:o 'martso] (March 8th) ; it isn't a real holiday, in the sense that people go to work and children go to school, but it is often celebrated by men giving a mimosa branch to the ladies.

→ Pasqua ['paskua]

At Easter Christian people go to the church (on Saturday night, or on Sunday) to celebrate Jesus Christ's resurrection. In the morning children are happy to get up, because they know they are going to open the UOVO DI PASQUA (the Easter egg) and then people have a great lunch with their relatives.

→ Lunedì dell'Angelo [lune'di del:'andʒelo] / Pasquetta [pa'skuet:a]

It is the day after Easter. Generally people celebrate it with friends and if the weather is nice, they generally enjoy a day in the countryside and have a picnic or eat at a barbecue.

→ La Festa della liberazione dal nazifascismo [la 'festa del:a libe'ratsione dal natsifa'ʃismo] /   Il 25 aprile [il venti'tʃinkue a'prile]

The "Festa della liberazione" is the Liberation Day in Italy: people celebrate the end of the second world war and the end of Nazi occupation of the country.

There are military parades in many cities, but especially in Rome, where the President of the Italian Republic visits the "Altare della Patria" honouring the so-called "Milite ignoto": the Tomb of the Unknown Soldier, to commemorate all soldiers killed in any war.

It is also the first occasion for people living close to the sea, to go to the beach with friends and   to get the first tun, and brave people have a quick dip, even if the water is a bit chilly; otherwise people often go to the countryside.

Post offices, banks, most stores and other businesses are closed.

→ Il 1° maggio [il 'primo 'madʒ:o] / la festa dei lavoratori [la 'festa dei lavora'tori]

Festa dei lavoratori: Labour day is May Day in Italy. May 1st is a public holiday dedicated to celebrate workers' right. It is also the occasion to meet friends, go to the beach or to the countryside.

Post offices, banks, most stores and other businesses are closed.

→ Il 2 giugno [il 'due 'dʒuɲo]

The "Festa della Repubblica" is the commemoration of the institutional referendum held by universal suffrage in 1946, in which the Italian people decided they wanted to have a Republic (12,717,923 votes) instead of a Monarchy (10,719,284). A grand military parade is organized in Rome and and there are important celebrations in all Italian embassies. As for the other holidays in late April and May, some people attend the parades and most of them often go to the sea or to the countryside with the family or friends.

Post offices, banks, most stores and other businesses are closed.

→ Ferragosto [fer:a'gosto]

On the 15th of August people celebrate the Assumption of Virgin Mary: "Assunzione di Maria". Christian people attend Mass and then everybody goes to the beach. This is time of vacation for nearly everybody, so many people are not at home, especially if they live in the North of Italy or in cities far from the sea, where the weather is really hot. A common practise is the "gavettone" [gave't:one]: teenagers play throwing cold water against each other.

→ Tutti i santi ['tut:i i 'santi] / Ognissanti [oɲi's:anti]

On November the 1st, many Italian honor the lives of their deceased relatives and all the saints (All Saints' Day). They visit special church services and place flowers on family graves.

→ Immacolata Concezione [im:ako'lata kontʃetsi'one]

On Dicember 8 people celebrate the Feast of the Immaculate Conception: the belief in the conception of the Blessed Virgin Mary in her mother's womb free from original sin. Christian people attend Mass, and everybody starts making the Christmas Tree (albero di Natale) and the Nativity scene (Presepe).

→ Natale [na'tale]

On Christmas Eve (Vigilia di Natale) people buy the last gifts and prepare a festive family meal (for the dinner of the Eve or the lunch of Christmas day... or even for both occasions!) On 24th December at night, or the next day in the morning, many people attend a special Mass.
At Christmas children get up early hoping to find many presents under their Christmas tree, and thank "Babbo Natale" (Santa Claus) for having been so good with them!
Families spend the rest of the day eating, chatting and playing bingo, cards and other board games.

→ Santo Stefano ['santo 'stefano]

This day is also known as "the second day (of Christmas)", "il secondo giorno" [il se'kondo 'dʒorno]. It is celebrated almost like Christmas: people take the occasion to have lunch with the same or some other relatives (if they have very big families), to play board games, and sometimes to go to the cinema with friends, in the afternoon or in the evening, to watch the new films, that often release at Christmas.

A Bite of Italian Flavour

When you think of Italy you inevitably also think of its cuisine. Everybody in the world knows what a PIZZA is or that it is difficult to eat SPAGHETTI. For Italian people, food is not just something to fill your stomach, but it is something related to culture, family and traditions.

Italian cuisine, following the principles of the Mediterranean diet, is very healthy. It makes an almost exclusive use of **extra virgin olive oil** (OLIO

EXTRA VERGINE D'OLIVA ['olio ekstra'verdʒine do'liva]), which is the healthiest fat.

"La colazione"

They generally eat from 3 to 5 times per day, starting from the COLAZIONE [kola'tsione], that is generally a very quick and light meal, especially in working days. Differently from the other meals, their breakfast is very different from other countries' breakfasts: Italian people generally eat sweet things, such as milk with biscuits, or some coffee or tea, or a cappuccino with a brioche, or bread and jam with some juice; no meat, no vegetables, no eggs!

Some people prefer to sleep longer and to have breakfast at the bar with a cappuccino or a coffee, and a pastry.

"La merenda"

The MERENDA, a small snack at school, is around 10:30 a. m., and children eat a piece of pizza or of focaccia bread, or a sweet snack and they drink some juice. Even adults sometimes have this break, and they call it "PAUSA CAFFÈ" ['pausa ka'f:æ]: it is the occasion to relax a bit, to chat with their colleagues and to calm down their stomach.

"Il pranzo"

Around 1 or 2 p. m. they have the main meal: IL PRANZO ['prandzo]. This is generally a very big meal, even if it is more and more common to eat less and faster, because of business reasons. In this case people may have a "piatto di pasta" ['piat:o di 'pasta] (plate of pasta), or   an "insalatona" [insala'tona] (mix salad), or just a "panino" [pa'nino] (sandwich). On holidays lunch is very different and especially if there is a particular occasion to celebrate it is a complex meal: they start with an
→ "Aperitivo" [aperi'tivo] (aperitif): enjoying a glass of Prosecco, with some peanuts and crisps; then they have the

→ "Antipasto" [anti'pasto] (appetizer). Here they have the most fanciful things, that may vary from region to region, but the classic Italian "antipasti" are: TAGLIERE DI AFFETTATI [ta'ʎere di af:e't:ati] (wooden cutting board with salami, raw ham, mortadella...), TAGLIERE DI FORMAGGI [ta'ʎere di for'madʒ:i] (wooden cutting board with cheese), BRUSCHETTA AL POMODORO [bru'sket:a al pomo'doro] (tomato bruschetta), OLIVE [o'live] (olives), CROSTINI [kro'stini] with pâté, or other kinds of creme, such as olives or artichokes crème, PROSCIUTTO E MELONE [pro'ʃut:o e me'lone] melon and ham, PIZZETTE [pi'ts:et:e] (small round pizza), CARPACCIO DI MARE [kar'patʃ:o di 'mare] (a dish of raw fish such as salmon, tuna or swordfish thinly sliced) or CARPACCIO DI TERRA [kar'patʃ:o di 'ter:a] (a dish of raw meat such as beef or veal thinly sliced or pounded thin).

Finally they arrive at the first course, even if often they may be already full!

→ "Primo" ['primo] (first course): it usually consists of a hot dish like PASTA ['pasta], RISOTTO [ri'sot:o], GNOCCHI ['ɲok:i], LASAGNE [la'saɲe] or a ZUPPA [dzup:a] (soup). The main sauces are: AL POMODORO [al pomo'doro] (tomato sauce), AL PESTO [al 'pesto] (pesto sauce), ALLA CARBONARA [al:a karbo'nara] (with bacon and egg), ALL'ARRABBIATA [al:ar:ab:i'ata] spicy tomato sauce, and AI QUATTRO FORMAGGI [ai ku'at:ro for'madʒ:i] (with four kinds of cheese).

→ "Secondo" [se'kondo] (second course / main course): this is generally CARNE ['karne] (meat) or PESCE ['peʃe] fish, and sometimes a TORTA SALATA ['torta sa'lata] (savoury pie). Veal, pork, chicken and turkey are most commonly used, though beef has become more popular since the Second World War and wild games, such as CINGHIALE [tʃingi'ale] (wild bore) and FAGIANO [fa'dʒano] (pheasant) are found particularly in Tuscany. Fish are frequently caught locally. Among seafood dishes we can also mention shellfish and octopus.

→ "Contorno" [kon'torno] (side dish). It may be a salad (INSALATA [insa'lata]) or cooked or raw vegetables such as FINOCCHI [fi'nok:i] (fennels), CAROTE [ka'rote] (carrots), POMODORI [pomo'dori] (tomatoes), PATATE [pa'tate] (potatoes), PISELLI [pi'sel:i] (peas) or FAGIOLI [fa'dʒoli] (beans). A traditional menu features salad along with the main course, and not at the beginning as a starter.

→ "Frutta" ['frut:a] (fruit). You may get a colourful MACEDONIA [matʃe'donia] (fruit salad), FRUTTA FRESCA ['frut:a 'freska] (fresh fruit) such as MELE ['mele] (apples), BANANE [ba'nane] (bananas), ARANCE [a'rantʃe] (oranges), ALBICOCCHE [albi'kok:e] (apricots), PESCHE ['peske] (peaches), ANGURIA [an'guria] (watermelon) and UVA ['uva] (grapes), depending on the season, or FRUTTA SECCA ['frut:a 'sek:a] (dried fruit), such as NOCI ['notʃi] (walnuts), MANDORLE [man'dorle] (almonds) and NOCCIOLE [no'tʃ:ole] (hazelnuts).

→ "Dolce" ['doltʃe] (dessert). This is the best part of the meal for many people, even if there is small space left! Typical deserts are TIRAMISÙ [tirami'su], CROSTATA [kro'stata] (tart) DI FRUTTA [di 'fru't:a] (fruit tart) or ALLA NUTELLA [al:a nutel:a] (nutella tart) and SORBETTO AL LIMONE [sor'bet:o al li'mone] (lemon sorbet).

But that's not all! They still need a

→ "Caffè" [ka'f:æ] (coffee). Note: Italian people will never have a cappuccino at this time of the day, but just an ESPRESSO [es'pres:o] or a CORRETTO for example ALLA SAMBUCA [ko'r:et:o al:a sam'buka] (coffee laced with Sambuca, or grappa or rum...); CAPPUCCINO is only meant for breakfast!

Now it is the best time for a

→ "Digestivo" [didʒe'stivo] (digestives): with the excuse they have eaten a lot, they think they have to drink some liqueurs to facilitate their digestion. The typical Italian AMMAZZACAFFÈ [am:ats:aka'f:æ] (literally "coffee killer") are the LIMONCELLO [limon'tʃel:o] (a liqueur made with lemon), VINSANTO E CANTUCCINI [vin'santo e kantutʃ:ini] (sweet white wine served with biscotti cookies, that may be dunked into the wine), GRAPPA ['grap:a], SAMBUCA [sam'buka] (anise flavoured liqueur), NOCINO [no'tʃino] (liqueur made with walnuts), AMARO [a'maro] (herbal liqueur).

After a lunch like this, it is hard to think of another snake, but the bravest, and generally the children, that never eat all the above mentioned things, have a second "merenda" around 4 p.m.

"La Cena"

Generally the Italian dinner is lighter than the lunch, if people have had time to eat enough at lunch. If there is a particular occasion, the organization and the menu may be the same as the one for lunch, otherwise people avoid to eat too many carbohydrates, leaving the first dish, and sometimes the dessert. After dinner it is even more common to drink a digestive, since you don't have to go back to work, but you just have to sleep or relax.

Test your Italian!

Exercise1: Complete the sentences with the right word; from the contest you may understand the meaning of the sentence, otherwise you can help yourself with a dictionary

11. Nel giardino fuori da …….. mia ho trovato una …… piena di monete d'oro.
12. Il …….. ha benedetto un bambino che faceva la ………. .
13. Mentre giocavo a calcio con i miei amici ho tirato la …….. addosso a una …….. che è cascata in testa a un mio amico.
14. ……… Luca, voglio raccontarti di quando mio nonno andava dalla campagna in città su di un piccolo ……… trainato dai cavalli.
15. Fra tutti i fiori la ………. ………. è la mia preferita.

Exercise 2: While you study Italian, each time you notice a couple of words like those you have just studied, write them down on an exercise book, try to identify the two meanings, and to pronounce them in the right way: with and without the double letter. Then try to remember them!

Exercise 3: Put the words in the correct order.

11) MIO BELLO CANE IL
12) TUA LA ROSSA   MACCHINA
13) LA GRANDE SORELLA MIA
14) TUOI CAPELLI I BIONDI
15) NOSTRA LA CASA SPAZIOSA
16) VOSTRO IL DIFFICILE   LAVORO
17) AMICO ITALIANO IL MIO
18) FACILE LINGUA MIA LA
19) LA FAMIGLIA BELLA VOSTRA
20) CITTÀ FAMOSA LA LORO

Exercise 4: Write the Italian name of the corresponding festivity

21. People celebrate Jesus' birth ....
22. People celebrate Jesus' resurrection ....
23. It is the end of the second world war in Italy ....
....
24. If you are good, the Befana will give you many sweets
....
25. Nobody works because it is Labour's day ....
or ....
26. Italian people celebrate the birth of the Italian Republic
....
27. Women are happier ....
28. Two days to celebrate the Virgin Mary: .... and
....
29. You   can   see   many   fireworks   everywhere
....
30. The day after Easter .... or
....
31. The day after Christmas ....
32. People often go to cemetery on this occasion ....
.... or ....

147

Exercise 5) Link the food to the correct kind of Italian meal

6. Pasta, meat, fruit and desert
7. Focaccia bread and orange juice
8. Milk and biscuits
9. Fish, fruit and digestive

A) MERENDA
B) CENA
C) PRANZO
D) COLAZIONE

Anwers:

Exercise 1

11. Nel giardino fuori da CASA mia ho trovato una CASSA piena di monete d'oro
12. Il PAPA ha benedetto un bambino che faceva la PAPPA
13. Mentre giocavo a calcio con i miei amici ho tirato la PALLA addosso a una PALA che è cascata in testa a un mio amico
14. CARO Luca, voglio raccontarti di quando mio nonno andava dalla campagna in città su di un piccolo CARRO trainato dai cavalli
15. Fra tutti i fiori la ROSA ROSSA è la mia preferita

Exercise 3

1) IL MIO CANE BELLO
2) LA TUA MACCHINA ROSSA
3) LA MIA SORELLA GRANDE
4) I TUOI CAPELLI BIONDI
5) LA NOSTRA CASA SPAZIOSA
6) IL VOSTRO LAVORO DIFFICILE
7) IL MIO AMICO ITALIANO
8) LA MIA LINGUA FACILE
9) LA VOSTRA FAMIGLIA BELLA
10) LA LORO CITTÀ FAMOSA

Exercise 4

1) Natale 2) Pasqua 3) Festa della Liberazione 4) Epifania 5) Il primo maggio / festa dei lavoratori 6) Festa della Repubblica 7) Festa della donna 8) Ferragosto and Immacolata Concezione 9) Capodanno 10) Lunedì dell'angelo or Pasquetta 11) Santo Stefano 12) Tutti I santi / Ognissanti

Exercise 5

1) - C) ; 2) - A)   , 3) - D) ; 4) - B)

Click Here to Check out the Rest of "*Italian For Tourists - The Most Essential Italian Guide to Travel Abroad, Meet People & Find Your Way Around*" on Amazon

Check Out My Other Books

Are you ready to exceed your limits? Then pick a book from the one below and start learning yet another new language.   I can't imagine anything more fun, fulfilling, and exciting!

If you'd like to see the entire list of language guides (there are a ton more!), go to:

>>**http://www.amazon.com/Dagny-Taggart/e/B00K54K6CS/**<<

About the Author

Dagny Taggart is a language enthusiast and polyglot who travels the world, inevitably picking up more and more languages along the way.

Taggart's true passion became learning languages after she realized the incredible connections with people that it fostered. Now she just can't get enough of it. Although it's taken time, she has acquired vast knowledge on the best and fastest ways to learn languages. But the truth is, she is driven simply by her motive to build exceptional links and bonds with others.

She is inspired everyday by the individuals she meets across the globe. For her, there's simply not anything as rewarding as practicing languages with others because she gets to make friends with people from all that come from a variety of cultures. This, in turn, has broadened her mind and thinking more than she would have ever imagined it could.

Of course, as a result of her constant travels, Taggart has become an expert on planning trips and making the most of time spent out of what she calls her "base" town. She jokes that she's practically at the nomad status now, but she's more content to live that way.

She knows how to live on a manageable budget weather she's in Paris or Phnom Penh. She knows how to seek out the adventures and thrills, no doubt, lying in wait at any city she visits. She knows that reflection on each every experience is significant if she wants to grow as a traveler and student of the world's cultures.

Because of this, Taggart chooses to share her understanding of languages and travel so that others, too, can experience the same life-altering benefits she has.

10232497R00085

Printed in Great Britain
by Amazon.co.uk, Ltd.,
Marston Gate.